INTERCULTURAL
COMMUNICATION
TRAINING

Communicating Effectively in Multicultural Contexts

Series Editors: William B. Gudykunst and Stella Ting-Toomey

Department of Speech Communication
California State University, Fullerton

The books in this series are designed to help readers communicate effectively in various multicultural contexts. Authors of the volumes in the series translate relevant communication theories to provide readable and comprehensive descriptions of the various multicultural contexts. Each volume contains specific suggestions for how readers can communicate effectively with members of different cultures and/ or ethnic groups in the specific contexts covered in the volume. The volumes should appeal to people interested in developing multicultural awareness or improving their communication skills, as well as anyone who works in a multicultural setting.

Volumes in this series

Intercultural Communication Training:
An Introduction

Richard Brislin
Tomoko Yoshida

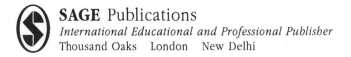

SAGE Publications
International Educational and Professional Publisher
Thousand Oaks   London   New Delhi

For information address:

 SAGE Publications, Inc.
2455 Teller Road
Thousand Oaks, California 91320

SAGE Publications Ltd.
6 Bonhill Street
London EC2A 4PU
United Kingdom

SAGE Publications India Pvt. Ltd.
M-32 Market
Greater Kailash I
New Delhi 110 048 India

Printed in the United States of America

Library of Congress Cataloging-in-Publication Data

Brislin, Richard W., 1945-
    Intercultural communication training: an introduction / Richard Brislin, Tomoko Yoshida.
        p. cm. — (Communicating effectively in multicultural context ; 2)
    Includes bibliographical references and index.
    ISBN 0-8039-5074-8. — ISBN 0-8039-5075-6 (pbk.)
    1. Cross-cultural orientation. 2. Intercultural communication.
I. Yoshida, Tomoko. II. Title. III. Series.
GN345.65.B77   1994
303.48'2—dc20   93-43061

94 95 96 97 98 10 9 8 7 6 5 4 3 2

Sage Production Editor: Astrid Virding

Contents

Preface

While predictions about the future are always difficult, one can be made with certainty. People will find themselves in large numbers of interactions where intercultural communication skills will be essential. Reasons include increasing amounts of contact brought on by overseas assignments in the business world, the movement of college students spending time in other countries, and increasing amounts of international travel among tourists. Other reasons relate to social changes within any one large and complex nation: affirmative action, the movement of immigrants and refugees, bilingual education programs, and movement away from the goal that ethnic minorities become part of a "melting pot."

Programs exist to prepare people for increasing amounts of intercultural contact and for encouraging the development of communication skills. The purpose of this book is to introduce readers to the study of intercultural communication training through coverage of central topics such as program assumptions, needs analysis, program content, evaluation, and practical advice for working with organizations whose executives might sponsor training. In preparing this book, we have drawn from more than 40 years of research dealing with intercultural communication theory and its application in training programs. In addition, we have drawn from the experiences of respected trainers who have a great deal of wisdom to share concerning how best to move from theory to practice.

As with many books that introduce readers to a fast moving field, our problem was not finding relevant published material but rather making choices from the extensive number of books, chapters, journal articles, and technical reports that deal with intercultural communication training. We wish, especially, that we could have written more about three areas: needs assessment, various training methods, and concepts that people can learn in training that move them toward increased intercultural sensitivity. In the chapter on needs assessment, we cite a number of texts and reference books where more information can be found. For training methods and concepts to be covered in training, we can refer readers to another book from Sage Publications with which we were involved. In the book *Improving Intercultural Interactions: Modules for Cross-Cultural Training Programs* (1994, edited by R. Brislin and T. Yoshida), 11 experienced trainers share information on the methods they use and the content they cover in a wide variety of programs. The modules (or collections of training materials) they share deal with international business, youth exchange programs, international students, counselors, teachers working in school systems with a multicultural student body, language interpreters, language teachers, health care professionals, and social service workers. In addition, the modules deal with issues that can be integrated into a variety of specific training programs, such as gender relations, nonverbal behavior, differing views of reality, and the cultural differences brought on by socialization into an individualistic compared to a collectivist culture.

The certainty that people will face the necessity of increasing their intercultural communication skills can be looked upon with dread or with enthusiasm. People who are wary of intercultural communication can point to the mistakes they will certainly make, the challenges to their pre-existing views, and the stress they will experience when they find that their good intentions are misunderstood. While recognizing these strong possibilities, other people will point to the stimulation that challenges to pre-existing viewpoints can bring and to the contributions that culturally diverse individuals can make in organizations where effective communication is the norm. We hope that readers of this book share our view that people can participate in intercultural communication training programs that both increase their skills and encourage them to reap the benefits that effective communication can bring.

–Richard W. Brislin
–Tomoko Yoshida
Honolulu, Hawaii

1

An Introduction to Programs, Goals, and Needs Assessment for Training

◆ The Great Wait

Fakir was a graduate student from India enrolled at one of the large universities in the American midwest. He arrived at his school in early August of last year and checked in with the international students' office to make sure his student visa was in order. He was told that there would be an orientation program for international students from August 5 to 12 during which participants would learn about, and even obtain some firsthand experience in, skills that would help in their adjustment to the United States and to graduate school. Fakir turned down the opportunity to participate, saying to himself that "I'm an adult who worked hard for my first degree in India. What major problems could there be working toward another degree?" He also wanted to visit his cousin at a school in a neighboring state prior to the start of classes on August 15.

Over the course of his first year in graduate school, Fakir was one of the better students in terms of his written work and the grades he received. Professors even pointed to him as one of the department's sharpest students. There was one aspect of his studies, however, that was causing problems. He did not

1

seem able to set up a committee of faculty members who would guide him on his master's degree thesis work. Other students, mostly Americans, had set up their committees, and this was distressing to Fakir because he knew that he was receiving better grades than some of them. Fakir happened to visit the international students office (visa again!) and happened to find one of the advisers, a woman named Shirley, in a rare moment of relative calm. Shirley said, "Your visa situation looks fine. Is there anything else you'd like to talk about?" Fakir took this opportunity to tell about his problem in his department. Shirley replied, "It's a fairly common complaint that I hear. Some people explain it this way. Many students from South Asia expect a professor to call them in and to tell them what thesis topics to consider. These students come from cultures in which students are expected to be highly deferential to a professor's wishes. The American professors, on the other hand, expect graduate students to come in and to propose a set of ideas that might be investigated. The American professors come from a culture in which individual initiative from a graduate student is appreciated. It's sometimes called 'the great wait.' The international graduate student is waiting for the professors to call him or her into their offices. The American professors are waiting for the student to make an appointment and to propose ideas. My recommendation is to write down what ideas you might want to study and to then make an appointment with a professor who may be interested in those or similar ideas."

Fakir responded emotionally, "This all makes sense. Why didn't someone tell me earlier?" Shirley bit her tongue and did not point out that Fakir had turned down an invitation to attend a cross-cultural training program a year earlier.

◆ Intercultural Communication and Cross-Cultural Training

Intercultural communication training refers to formal efforts designed to prepare people for more effective interpersonal relations when they interact with individuals from cultures other than their own (Carbaugh, 1990; Paige, 1992). These efforts are most frequently encountered as part of *cross-cultural training* programs, or formal, well-planned, budgeted, and staffed programs designed to prepare for the wide variety of issues people face when adjusting to another culture (Bhawuk, 1990; Brislin, 1989; Brislin & Pedersen, 1976; Landis & Brislin, 1983). The terms are often used interchangeably. One reason is that it is hard to think of cross-cultural adjustment issues that do not involve communication among people. Even if adjustment issues such as housing, climate, and transportation are covered, there will be communication issues involving interactions with landlords, merchants, and ticket agents as people deal with the issues in other cultures. The other reason for the frequent interchangeability of terms is that attitudes and skills directly related to intercultural communication are strongly related to people's overall adjustment to, and satisfaction with, their work in other cultures (Gudykunst & Hammer, 1984; Hammer, 1989). In this book, we will be drawing from the published literature on both intercultural communication and cross-cultural training, and we will be emphasizing those aspects of training that explicitly involve face-to-face communication among people. The guidelines for establishing good training are applicable to a wide variety of programs for people working in a country other than the one in which they hold citizenship (e.g., the graduate student from India studying in the United States). They are also applicable to programs that prepare people from one cultural background to interact with members of another when all live in the same country (e.g., African Americans interacting with Anglos in the workplace).

◆ Various Target Audiences for Intercultural Communication Training

The field of intercultural communication training has developed extensively since World War II. Reasons include the continuing increases in the already large numbers of students who seek out educational opportunities in countries other than their own; increased air travel; the development of a global marketplace; increasing sensitivities to gender and ethnic differences in the workplace; the movement of immigrants and refugees; the development of programs aimed at person-to-person contact (Peace Corps, Youth Exchange Programs); and others. Examples of programs for a variety of target audiences, all using the same basic approaches that will be reviewed in Chapters 2 through 5 of this book, allow examination of the range of intercultural experiences that people have today and will continue to have into the 21st century. The list of programs emphasizes work done since about 1982, given the existence of books that reviewed programs carried out prior to that year (Brislin & Pedersen, 1976; Landis & Brislin, 1983). Programs have been established for these and other audiences:

1. International students who work toward degrees in countries other than their own (Mabe, 1989; Miller, 1989);
2. Adolescents who spend a significant amount of time living with a family in another culture (Cushner, 1989);
3. The Peace Corps, consisting of volunteers who are assigned to work on various community projects in other countries (Barnes, 1985);
4. Health care workers, including counselors, physicians, and nurses who deal with a multicultural clientele (Berry, Kessler, Fodor, & Wato, 1983; Day, 1990; Heath, Neimeyer, & Pedersen, 1988; Kristal, Pennock, Foote, & Trygstad, 1983; Lefley, 1984);
5. Social workers working with clients from cultural backgrounds other than their own (Jones, 1983; Montalvo, Lasater, & Valdez, 1982);
6. Refugees, especially from Southeast Asia, seeking help in their adjustment to cultural differences in education, medical care, housing, and social services (Center for Applied Linguistics, 1982; Redick & Wood, 1982; Williams, 1985);
7. Technical assistant advisers, usually from highly industrialized nations, assigned to project development in less industrialized countries (Bussom, Elsaid, Schermerhorn, & Wilson, 1984);

8. Overseas businesspeople and international traders seeking joint agreements and sales of products and services (Aranda, 1986; Bogorya, 1985; Inman, 1985; Rippert-Davila, 1985);

9. Elementary school children having difficulties interacting with age peers from other cultures (Bergsgaard & Larsonn, 1984; Esquivel & Keitel, 1990);

10. School counselors, and other school personnel, in multicultural communities (Carey, Reinart, & Fontes, 1990; Gonzalez, 1985; Laughlin, 1984; Webb, 1990);

11. Job seekers in the United States who have limited English language proficiency (Buchanan, 1990);

12. Native Americans seeking job counseling in their search for employment outside reservations (McShane, 1987; Runion & Gregory, 1984);

13. White Australians living in rural areas and interacting frequently with Aboriginal Australians (Davidson, Hansford, & Moriarty, 1983);

14. Tourists seeking out intercultural understanding as part of their vacations (Fisher & Price, 1991);

15. Personnel officers in large organizations seeking programs for managers who deal with subordinates of the other gender (Berryman-Fink & Fink, 1985);

16. Diplomats, or others representing their governments, assigned to other countries (Marquardt & Hempstead, 1983).

There are several commonalties in this wide-ranging list of audiences for programs, and these commonalities form the basis of any book like the present one that provides an introduction to intercultural communication training. The commonalities include (a) the necessity of establishing good interpersonal relations with people, and (b) communicating effectively in the presence of cultural differences that can interfere with good relations. At times, the reasons for communication difficulties are totally invisible to people since they are part of their socialization as to what is "correct and proper" in their own culture. Recall the incident that introduced this chapter: Fakir was socialized to wait for a call from his professors. Shirley pointed out another culture's norm is that people should show initiative and should approach people in authority with their suggestions.

People rarely have the opportunity to examine their socialization and to ask "why" certain behaviors are considered correct in their culture. This can be done in good training programs. Other commonalities are that people want to accomplish goals in their dealings with people from other cultures (e.g., degrees for international students, sales for international traders), and they want to experience as little stress as possible while doing so. These commonalities lead to a discussion of four goals commonly found in intercultural communication training programs.

◆ The Goals of Training Programs

When examined carefully, most good training programs incorporate at least four goals that are all related to people's adjustment and effectiveness (Bhawuk, 1990; Brislin, 1989; Hammer, 1989). In the examples used to clarify points, we will most often refer to overseas assignments, although very similar examples could be put forth that deal with intercultural communication within any one large country.

ENJOYMENT AND BENEFIT

The first goal is that people should be exposed to training materials and exercises that will increase the enjoyment they experience and the benefits they receive. *Enjoyment* refers to a sense of happiness and excitement such that people look forward to getting up in the morning and going to work. Rather than simply tolerating an unpleasant interruption in their lives, people should feel enthusiastic about their intercultural interactions and the stimulation they can bring. At times, a sense of active enjoyment is very difficult and the goals of training should then focus on *benefits*. For example, married international students from Asia often leave their families behind and travel to North America or Europe for 4 or more years of study. The experience is admittedly difficult given the absence of their families and the 80- to 90-hour workweeks they choose to set for themselves so that they can return home as soon as possible. In cases like this, training can focus on benefits such as the quality of graduate instruction and guidance in developing effective work relationships with professors and fellow graduate students. Because good intercultural relationships (whether work oriented, interpersonal, or both) are central to adjustment (Gudykunst & Hammer, 1984; Hammer, 1989), suggestions for developing these relationships are central to training. One way to measure program success is to ask people, after they have actually begun their assignments, if they have developed intercultural relationships. Questions can deal with how much voluntary free time is spent with people from the host culture, and how many hosts can be called upon in times of need.

THE ATTITUDES OF HOSTS TOWARD SOJOURNERS

An aspect of the first goal, then, is that sojourners should report good relations with hosts. The second goal reminds us that sojourner self-reports are not enough: feelings about positive relations must be reciprocated by hosts. If attention is given to the combination of goals (1) and (2), then there is the possibility of identifying a type of person with whom most readers are probably familiar. This is the type of person who reports that he or she has many friends and who can list their names. If the people on the list are interviewed, they say that the person is obnoxious, difficult to get along with, and thoroughly conceited to think that the list represents the names of friends.

Research in intercultural communication has demonstrated the importance of positive interpersonal relations. Hawes and Kealey (1981) carried out research on the experiences of technical assistance advisers from Canada working in a number of less industrialized nations. In addition to interviewing the advisers, they also asked questions of the hosts with whom the advisers were working closely (sometimes called "counterparts"). Hawes and Kealey found that, after the advisers returned home to Canada, some were remembered more positively than others. The advisers who were remembered favorably had established good interpersonal relationships with counterparts so that they could transfer the technological skills they knew. The transfer of skills is especially important since these can be some of the "products left behind" by visiting sojourners. For example, assume the technical assistance advisers were sent to build sanitation facilities. The advisers who were remembered as the most successful transferred their engineering skills so that counterparts could both maintain existing facilities and build others. A fact that must be constantly kept in mind is that most sojourners return to their home countries. In addition to leaving behind the visible products of their efforts, such as roads, buildings, and written policies, they can also leave behind the less visible skills that allow these products to be created. The development of positive interpersonal relationships allows skills transfer to take place.

PEOPLE'S OWN GOALS

Any discussion of skill transfer made possible by good interpersonal relationships leads to considerations of a third goal of training. Good training programs provide information that will help people achieve their goals. Very few sojourners live in other cultures without very explicit goals. Even those who seem simply to be taking time out from their careers and experiencing life elsewhere have the goal of encountering and dealing with cultural differences, finding stimulation, having the opportunity to rethink their lives in their own culture, and so forth. Goals are more obvious for other types of sojourners. International students want to obtain their degrees within a reasonable amount of time. Overseas businesspeople want to establish joint trade agreements. Technical assistance advisers want to complete development projects and, if they are sensitive to the issues raised above, want to transfer their skills. Health care workers want to deliver the best medical care possible. Social workers want their clients to benefit from social services for a certain amount of time, but they also want their clients to develop the skills necessary to become independent of tax-supported social services. Given their knowledge of trainee goals, program developers can choose training methods to communicate information and skills relevant to goal accomplishment. International students working in the United States can be introduced to skills that might be infrequently used in their own country, such as showing initiative in the selection of research topics, speaking up in seminars, occasionally disagreeing with professors, preparing term papers and theses in an acceptable style, and so forth. Overseas businesspeople from North America working in Asia can be introduced to cultural differences in the appropriateness of "getting down to business" in contrast to spending time in engaging in small talk so that interpersonal trust can be established. Let's continue with this example to see the range of information and skills that can be introduced. In role-playing exercises (to be discussed more fully in Chapters 5 and 6 of this book), trainees can play the parts of overseas businesspeople and hosts, sometimes engaging in extensive small talk (as appropriate in the host culture) and sometimes getting down to business quickly and consequently losing contracts. Frequently, people are not only expected to participate in extensive small talk, they are also expected to participate in many social encounters in restaurants and well-known tourist spots. Whenever possible, the exact reasons for the different behaviors should be discussed. In this case (and as discussed more fully in Triandis, Brislin, & Hui, 1988), extensive small talk and frequent social encounters become a substitute for lawyers. There are far fewer lawyers in Asian countries than in the United States or Canada. In Asia, if problems in a contract arise, businesspeople want to get on the phone with their colleagues, arrange a face-to-face meeting, and cooperate in the development of a solution. How do they know this can be done? They know because they only enter into business relationships with people they trust and with whom they are comfortable. They develop this trust by spending long periods of time getting to know other people, entertaining them, engaging in various social encounters with them, and so forth. Even though the time and money spent on entertaining overseas businesspeople may seem costly, hosts know that the money involved is much less than what would be spent on lawyers. Asians do not want to deal with another country's lawyers. They want to solve problems cooperatively, and the long periods of time getting to know potential business partners are necessary so that a judgment about "future cooperativeness" can be made.

STRESS REDUCTION

One of the assumptions of good cross-cultural training programs is that if trainees are well prepared to deal with the differences that they will surely encounter, then stress will be reduced. Dealing with stress should be one of training's explicit goals. Cross-cultural assignments mean that people are removing themselves from the familiar environments in which they have learned to obtain the goals that they desire. In familiar environments, they know how to enter their children into school, find housing, negotiate with co-workers, start a checking account, and so forth. The fact that they have to do these tasks in unfamiliar settings and with unfamiliar people is anxiety arousing and stressful (Berry, 1990). Stress, in turn, can lead to threats to people's health (Ilola, 1990). The most commonly used term in intercultural communication training is probably *culture shock,* the set of emotions that results from having the familiar structures of one's own culture taken away. People cannot figure out how to obtain their goals in this other place. "They can't understand the jokes I tell! I never know when a promise has been made concerning a possible agreement that they have been discussing! They seem to be less than straightforward when they have something to say! And they seem to be talking about me all the time!"

When stress is explicitly addressed in training, the goal should be its reduction rather than its elimination. Stress is an

inevitable part of many jobs and cannot realistically be elimi-
nated. For example, the job of air traffic controller is stressful.
If skilled professionals were to accept the task of introducing
new technologies for traffic control in other countries, they
might decide that a good approach would be to work side-by-
side with trainees in actual job settings. This will involve a great
deal of stress because control over the safe landing of aircraft
is such an important job. The goal of cross-cultural training
should be to prepare sojourners so that they experience no
more stress than they would holding down similar jobs in their
own country. Similar arguments can be made about the stress
faced by international students. As most readers will agree,
thinking back to their own years in school, the job of college
students is stressful. The goal for training programs aimed at
international students would be to present information and
skills so that they would experience no more stress than if they
were studying in their own culture.

   In actual programs, training methods have been borrowed
from the more general techniques of stress reduction: relaxation, exercise, restructuring personal thoughts so that they are
less harmful, nurturance of hobbies, and so forth (Brislin,
Cushner, Cherrie, & Yong, 1986). Other experts suggest training techniques that will increase people's observational skills
so that they can discover accurate information as they deal with
problems during their actual intercultural experiences. For example, returning to the anecdote used at the very beginning of
this chapter, the staff of a training program might have encouraged Fakir to observe what the most successful graduate students in his department actually do. If he had done so, he might
have discovered on his own that the successful students made
appointments with professors and suggested a range of ideas
for their own theses. Gao and Gudykunst (1990) suggest:

   By observing host nationals, describing their observations, search-
   ing out alternative interpretations for the behavior observed, and
   deciding on the culturally appropriate interpretation, trainees can

continually increase their knowledge of the host culture throughout their stay. This increased knowledge, in turn, will reduce
their uncertainty and anxiety, which, in turn, will increase their
adaptation. (p. 314)

If they keep these four goals in mind, trainers will be making
a good start in their task of developing an effective program (more
on stress in Chapter 3).

◆ Needs Assessment

Trainers will further their chances of success if they conduct
a needs assessment of what trainees expect given their participation in a program. Although there are exceptions (e.g., Albert,
1985; Dotlich, 1982; Wood & Mallinckrodt, 1990), needs assessment is not as frequently discussed in the intercultural communication training literature as it should be. The published literature suggests the typical procedure is that trainers receive an
offer to develop a program in an organization. They then determine the amount of time they will have and agree on a budget
with a representative of the organization. Then the trainers put
together a collection of methods (with probable time allotments
for each) with which they are comfortable. While this may
seem a reasonable approach, the needs, desires, wishes, and
preferences of trainees are badly underemphasized.

Given the relative paucity of discussion of needs assessment
in intercultural communication, we will be turning to the
general literature on training for guidance (e.g., Goldstein, 1991;
Schneier, Guthrie, & Olian, 1988; Swierczek & Carmichael,
1985). As mentioned in the preface to this book, there are three
topics that we wish we had more space to discuss. This is one
of them, and because our discussion can only introduce this
important area, we recommend that the sources cited (especially the extensive treatment by Goldstein, 1991) be consulted.

◆ Some Methods for Needs Assessment

Needs assessments enable trainers to obtain information about the people who will be participating and about the organization in which they work. With the help of this information, program developers can make choices about the content and training techniques they will actually use in putting together the program. We will cover four methods commonly used in needs assessment, and we will then suggest a combination of methods that we have personally found helpful in designing training programs for a number of different audiences.

OBSERVATION

Using observational methods, members of the training staff (hereafter "trainers," for convenience) visit the organization and obtain information by watching and listening carefully. For example, they can observe issues such as the number of staff available for the demands of the workload, with special attention to aspects of the workload that involve intercultural communication. Examples would be the number of foreign student advisers in a university given the number of international students, or the amount of international telephone traffic in a trading company. Many times, careful observations will lead to recommendations that do not deal with training and that remind all concerned that not all problems can be addressed through training alone. If an organization's management is concerned that people in different departments do not communication very frequently, they might bring in specialists to give workshops on communication skills. However, observations might reveal that there are few places where people across departments might meet and have opportunities to communicate. Is there a lounge where people can take breaks? Is there a lunchroom, or do people have to scatter to nearby restaurants? Is the mailroom big enough so that people might chat there when checking their daily mail? Trainers should often take on the broader role of "consultant" and feel comfortable making a wide-ranging set of recommendations.

The advantages of observational methods is that trainers can obtain information firsthand and develop a program that takes the actual day-to-day demands on people into account. Trainers develop a great deal of credibility when they successfully communicate to program participants that they know the problems people face on a day-to-day basis. Disadvantages are that observational methods are time consuming and expensive in terms of staff time. Given that trainers want to make a living in their professions, many simply will not be able to afford the time that careful observation demands. If they assign younger individuals to carry out the observations, the experienced trainers will have to take pains to see that some common mistakes are not made. One common mistake, for example, is to make conclusions based on superficial first impressions of people and their organizations. Another mistake is to focus on the most colorful or attention-grabbing event, such as an argument between two people. Such an event may be very trivial considering the total range of behaviors that might have been observed. Another disadvantage is that observers do not have a clear role in the minds of those being observed. It is easy for observers to be mistaken for spies, or for efficiency experts who will be redesigning people's familiar work routines.

INTERVIEWS

Trainers can develop a set of about 10 questions and ask them of people in the organization. Why 10 questions? There are always limits on the time of busy people, and trainers do not want to wear out their welcome by tiring the interviewees who are kind enough to set their own work aside. We also recommend that trainers have the questions memorized, and are prepared to omit certain questions if the information has already been obtained. Many times, after being asked one question, people will give answers to two or three that are on the trainer's list. For example, one question might deal with commonly experienced communication problems when people are from different cultural backgrounds. In responding, a given individual will often answer other questions that were to be asked about stress, counterparts, or gender differences. If the trainer has these questions memorized, he or she will realize that answers have already been given and consequently some of the other questions need not be asked. Or, if more information is desired, the trainer can say: "You already referred to stressful communications in response to an earlier question. Is there anything else about stress that you'd like to tell me?" If trainers ask questions that have already been answered, or do not recognize that partial answers have already been given, interviewees become irritated and often conclude that the trainer is either too rigid or not very well prepared.

The advantages of interviews are that they are very flexible. Trainers can carry out interviews within the organization, over the phone, or at a neutral site outside the organization. Interviews allow trainers to become acquainted with some of the same people with whom they will be interacting during the actual training program. Interviews, in sharp contrast to questionnaires, allow people to express themselves in their own preferred way. They can use their own vocabulary, their own communication style, and can take the opportunity to ignore a trainer's question and respond to another question that they formulate for themselves. The disadvantages are that it is sometimes hard to summarize the results of interviews, given that different people answer questions in so many different ways. Another disadvantage is that interviewees can easily become self-conscious and may fear retributions from an organization's management if they give answers that are overly candid. Skillful interviews can often put people at ease and can set up a data-recording system that insures confidentially, but skillful interviewers may have to be paid a salary that exceeds the trainer's budget.

KEY CONSULTATION

Any discussion of interviewing leads to the question, "Who will be interviewed?" One needs assessment method that Goldstein (1991) suggests is called key consultation. Using this approach, people are selected because they should have information useful in the development of training programs. We argue that key consultation is especially appropriate for intercultural communication training. One of the most difficult problems trainers face is that intercultural communication is so unfamiliar to many people. In contrast to other types of training where the purpose is immediately clear (public speaking for salespeople, the latest word processing system for technical writers), the need for intercultural communication training is often not immediately obvious. In contrast, people who have actually had to communicate across cultural boundaries are more likely to feel the need for training. For example, if counselors accustomed to interacting with people much like themselves suddenly find themselves working with refugees who have recently arrived from another country, then these counselors will inevitably experience communication difficulties. They will likely be receptive to a good program aimed at the special needs of cross-cultural counselors (Pedersen, 1988). Writing about his work with businesspeople involved in international ventures, Hofstede (1980) discusses this important issue in a similar manner.

> My general experience [working with many businesspeople] is that the amount of international exposure within the group strongly affects the way the subject [of training] is received. Internationally experienced audiences have little trouble seeing its importance and tolerating a certain amount of introspection into their own cultural constraints. Internationally naive audiences have difficulty seeing the points, and some members even feel insulted when their own culture is discussed. (p. 9)

When recommending the careful interviewing of key informants, we are taking advantage of some research findings derived from work with people who have had previous intercultural experiences (Brislin, 1981; Useem & Useem, 1967). Many people who have lived in another culture, or who have interacted extensively with people from other cultural backgrounds, become interested in the special issues of intercultural communication. They have learned, because of their own firsthand experience, that (a) intercultural communication can lead to emotional reactions when people are misunderstood and that (b) people have to modify their behavior if they are to communicate effectively. Further, they (c) enjoy interacting with others who have had intercultural experiences and (d) are comfortable talking about the special problems that intercultural contact can bring. The finding (c) that people who had extensive intercultural contact seek each other out is especially interesting. They do not necessarily have the same type of experience in common and they have not necessarily lived in the same country. That is, the daughter of missionary parents assigned to China may become friends with the son of businesspeople who worked in Sweden. What do they have in common? They know what adjustment to another culture entails. They know the modifications people have to make to communicate effectively across culture boundaries. They know firsthand what terms like *culture shock* and *stressful intercultural experiences* mean. Of course, not all people who have had intercultural experiences have these interests. Some people who have lived in another country for 2 years, for example, may as well have stayed home because they learned next to nothing. Keeping this possibility in mind, our experience has been that 75% to 80% of people who have had extensive intercultural experiences make good key informants in needs assessments.

Our advice, then, is to seek out interculturally experienced people in organizations whose leaders are requesting training programs. Here's how the identification of experienced people might work in practice. Someone from an organization contacts the trainer. After agreeing about the possibility of developing a program the trainer asks, "Who might I talk to about the expectations and needs of the people who will be in the program?

Are there people who have worked for a long time in other countries? Or are there people who have worked with people from various cultural backgrounds in their own country?" As a result of these questions, the trainer should obtain the names of people who have experienced the sorts of interactions summarized earlier: people who spent a year abroad as students, recent immigrants, members of ethnic minority groups, people whose childhood involved years spent abroad because of their parents' job assignments, and so forth. We assume that two or three people can be identified in this way. Then, once these people are contacted, the trainer can ask "Who else besides you in this organization has worked extensively with people from other cultures?" Given that people with these experiences interact with each other, more names should be forthcoming. These people can then be interviewed in a manner similar to that already discussed.

QUESTIONNAIRES USING A DELPHI PROCEDURE

Once information is obtained from key informants, their statements can be made into questionnaire items to which larger numbers of people can respond. Upon seeing and responding to the questionnaire items, this larger number of people is also invited to comment freely in writing. The procedure known as Delphi (e.g., used by Cogswell & Stubblefield, 1988) involves the circulation of questionnaire responses and comments over a series of rounds.

For example, assume that a key informant recommends, "I think that any training should actually allow people to practice changing some of their typical behaviors that are irritating to people in other cultures." From this suggestion, the trainer could develop the following questionnaire items:

- The training program should allow me to identify some of the reasons why people in my culture behave the way that they do.

strongly agree   agree   no opinion   disagree   strongly disagree

- The training program should allow me to identify reasons why some of my behaviors will not be appropriate in other cultures.

strongly agree   agree   no opinion   disagree   strongly disagree

- The training program should allow me to practice changes in my behavior so that my behavior will be more appropriate in the other culture.

strongly agree   agree   no opinion   disagree   strongly disagree

Note that some of the behaviors referred to, that are more and less appropriate given cultural influences, have already been discussed. In the incident used to introduce this chapter, Fakir learns that one of his typical behaviors is to wait for direction from his professors. It is more appropriate in the United States for him to modify this behavior and to initiate interaction with his professors.

The responses to questionnaire items, as well as people's free comments, are then circulated to everyone who might be in the training program. All are asked to respond to the ideas and training recommendations made. After these comments are summarized by the training director, the materials (with emphasis on what would be covered during training) are circulated again. Given time limitations, a Delphi procedure continuing for three rounds is usually adequate to obtain reactions from the people in the organization. The advantages to this approach are that all are allowed to "have their say." Especially if they see that their views were taken into account, people are likely to feel appreciative that the trainers have taken steps to meet their needs. People may also have a sense of personal investment in the training program if their views are taken into account. A further advantage is that the Delphi process can stimulate people's memories and remind them of a concern that they might not have expressed on their own. For example, one respondent might be concerned about time for questions and answers during training, but might forget to mention this if asked a direct question about desires for the program. But if this respondent, as part of the Delphi process, sees that someone else raised the issue of questions and answers, he or she can write down, "I also think this is necessary!" A disadvantage is that many people feel that answering questionnaires puts constraints on the way they want to express themselves. Although trainers might then point to the additional possibility that people write their reactions in their own words, many will say that such a procedure favors the opinions of people who are skillful in communicating their ideas through writing. If a key informant in the organization has the trust of many people, the trainer can often suggest that oral recommendations can be funneled through that central person.

◆ The Use of Key Informants in Practice

Because we are recommending the use of key informants in needs assessment, we would like to present some typical responses we have recorded during our own interviews. Over the past few years we have been asked to develop programs for a number of audiences, and we will focus on three examples here:

1. counselors in mental health clinics who have clients from various cultural backgrounds;
2. student personnel administrators, in colleges and universities, who deal with large numbers of international students; and
3. businesspeople in organizations seeking expansion into international ventures.

After agreeing to develop a program, we have asked the person who contacted us to give us the names of some people who have had international and/or extensive intercultural experience. We have always been given at least three names, and we have obtained others by asking those individuals from the original list of nominees. We then ask them questions such as the following. We have obtained the sorts of responses that we include here for each of the three types of training audiences.

Question: "What are the sorts of issues that individuals in the organization will face given that they will be interacting with people from other cultural backgrounds?"

Answer from a counselor. "I think it will be stressful for counselors to deal with people from so many different groups, one right after the other. One hour, they'll deal with a refugee family. Then, a member of a minority group from the inner city. Then, a woman coming up against a glass ceiling in trying to get promoted. It will be almost impossible to know enough about everyone's cultural background to be helpful."

Answer from a student personnel administrator. "International students often don't come in to an office with their problems until the problems are so large that they are almost impossible to deal with. They tend to rely on other students from their own country, and if all are somewhat ignorant of good ways to deal with problems in this country, then the blind may end up leading the blind."

Answer from a businessperson. "Especially in contacts that just can't last for long periods of time, as in phone conversations dealing with orders and delivery dates, it may be hard for people to understand when a firm deal has been finalized. One party may say something polite but noncommittal, and that may be very proper according to his or her cultural norms. But if the other party interprets the polite response as a deal-maker, then bad feelings can result."

Question: "What will people have to do differently (for example, what familiar behaviors will they have to change) given increased intercultural contract?"

Answer from a counselor. "When a client talks about something with which counselors are unfamiliar, they have to become comfortable asking clients to explain it. Counselors have to overcome the fear that clients will think they are ignorant. Clients are looking for concern, empathy, and a desire to help. They will forgive a lack of knowledge about specific aspects of their culture as long as they see these traits in counselors."

Answer from a student personnel administrator. "International students often take a long time to communicate the real problem that brought them into the adviser's office. Often, they will tell about something that is not really the main problem, and the adviser has to encourage the student to explain what is really on his or her mind. This is one reason why the work hours of international student advisers are so long. If a student comes in at 4:15 P.M., the adviser is unwise to make an appointment for later in the week. The student wants to talk right then and there!"

Answer from a businessperson. "For American businesspeople, many will find that relationships have to be nurtured and maintained more than with business contacts in their own country. Many Asians, for instance, do not make as sharp a distinction between 'people in my network' and 'people who are friends.' If Americans do the sorts of things that they do with their friends, such as spending voluntary free time together, they will probably have better business dealings."

Question: "Have there been other training programs in this organization recently—any kind of training? If so, what mistakes were made that we might avoid?" (Note: The purpose of this question is to discover what approaches to training are unpopular in the organization).

Answer from a counselor. "We had a workshop on DSM-III, the third version of the *Diagnostic and Statistical Manual of Mental Disorders,* which is a classification scheme that should assist counselors. I thought that the trainer was too defensive of the Manual and was unwilling to discuss cases that didn't fit neatly into the scheme."

Answer from a student personnel administrator. "One of the worst things is when trainers make sweeping generalizations about something, such as how to deal with college students. But they don't address the fact that they are working with generalizations and that there are always exceptions. Novice personnel administrators latch onto these generalizations since they are seeking 'quick fixes' to help them through their workload. Only later do they find out that a great deal of thought has to go into the decision concerning whether to use a generalization or not."

Answer from a businessperson. "We had a workshop on sexual harassment in the workplace recently. I got the feeling that the trainers had their 'stuff' and that they had presented the same content in other organizations dozens of time. They focused on what the courts have decided, and I'll admit that this was reasonable enough. But it meant that they did not answer questions about cases that would never enter the courts but can still cause problems in the workplace. For example, can I as a male suggest that a woman dress in a more conservative manner when dealing with people from some cultural backgrounds? Whether I do or don't will unlikely lead to a court case, but it can make for unpleasant relations if some kind of formal grievance is filed."

Question: "A large number of activities in cross-cultural training programs involve the very active participation of trainees. For example, people speak in front of others, they practice new behaviors, they engage in role-playing sessions, and so forth. Do you expect that there will be any resistance to these types of activities?"

Answer from a counselor. "I think that people will be willing to become actively involved. Counselors talk a great deal about 'developing counseling skills.' And they realize that this means practicing the skills. I would caution, however, that counselors (at least in this organization) want information and skills that will help them with their work with various clients. If the ideas presented in training do not have a clear and direct application to the work of counselors, they will not be well received."

Answer from a student personnel administrator. "It's a lively group of people who will be in the training program and so there should be no problem with activities such as role-playing. They know that, given the much larger number of foreign students who will be coming, that they will have many more sessions with students about their visas. You might use that fact as a starting point for various active exercises."

Answer from a businessperson. "The people here are so unfamiliar with anything that involves international contact that they will be very uncomfortable taking part in exercises where they are observed by others. They will probably want to sit quietly and be passive members of an audience for the material that the trainers present. And they will be very critical, constantly asking, 'Why is this stuff you are presenting so important?' "

◆ The Next Steps

After carrying out a needs assessment, the trainers should have a great deal of information about the types of people who will be in the program, what they expect, what they are willing to do during the program, and what pitfalls should be carefully avoided. The trainers can then make decisions about program content and methods given the guidance suggested by the needs assessment. Much of the program content will involve decisions about the three major aspects of intercultural communication:

1. awareness, knowledge, and information about culture, cultural differences, and the specific culture in which trainees will be living;
2. attitudes related to intercultural communication, such as people's feelings about others who are culturally different (e.g., tolerance, prejudice, or active enthusiasm about developing close relationships); and the emotional confrontation people experience when dealing with cultural differences in their everyday communication; and
3. skills, or new behaviors that will increase the chances of effective communication when living and/or working with people from other cultural backgrounds.

These three aspects of intercultural communication are the subjects of the next three chapters.

2

Awareness and Knowledge as Content Areas for Intercultural Communication Training

◆ **Working With Immigrants**

Mark and Susan have been dedicated members of the same church for many years. In addition to attending religious services, they have been actively involved in helping newly arrived church-sponsored immigrants settle into the community. Their generosity and enthusiasm have long been appreciated by John, the organizer of the immigrant program at their church. A concern, however, has been raised by the immigrant community with regard to volunteers such as Mark and Susan. The spokesperson for the immigrant community came in to see John last week.

> You know how much we *really* appreciate what all of you have done for us, don't you? Well, that has been one reason we haven't said anything so far, but it has gotten to the point that members of our community are starting to distrust members of your church. For example, many of your church volunteers seem to assume that not being able to speak English also means childlike intelligence. When one of the families asked why furniture is so expensive in this country, Mark actually started explaining that it is because

wood needs to be cut from trees and then processed, etc. Furniture in our country goes through the same process too, you know! Some families have also complained that many of your volunteers are very pushy about doing things the "American way." While one of my friends was washing her clothes by hand, Susan walked in and took the clothes from her hand and put them into the washing machine! Clothes are precious to us, so we like to take good care of them! What really seems to confuse most of the families, though, is why your volunteers seem to be so friendly and helpful in the beginning and then stop abruptly after about 6 months and start helping another family. Is friendship so fickle in America?

◆ Awareness, Knowledge, Emotions, and Skills

Once the needs assessment has been conducted and the problems as well as the program goals have been delineated, the trainer must now determine which approach to take. For the purposes of this book, we have chosen to combine two of the more commonly used approaches and to apply them to the special case of intercultural communication. These are the Awareness, Knowledge & Skills continuums (Sue, Bernier, Durran, Feinberg, et al., 1982) and the Knowledge, Attitude & Skills continuums (Knight, 1981). What we propose is a four-step approach: (1) Awareness, (2) Knowledge, (3) Emotions (includes attitudes), and (4) Skills (involving visible behaviors).

What distinguishes cross-cultural training from other types of training such as "computer usage training" and "airplane pilot training" is that the need to acquire skills is not as obvious. Because many trainees and sponsoring organizations do not feel a pressing need to learn effective cross-cultural communication skills, it is often necessary to spend a significant amount of time raising *awareness* of the importance of these skills. Another characteristic of cross-cultural training is that since complex interpersonal interactions are so central to its success, people's *emotions* need to be addressed as well. When these two additional steps are included in the more standard program focusing on *knowledge* and *skills,* many trainers run out of time, resulting in minimal coverage of one or more of the dimensions. The triple bind facing many cross-cultural trainers is that due to the additional steps (i.e., awareness and emotions), cross-cultural training necessarily is much more time consuming. As mentioned earlier, however, the need for intercultural communication competence is not as apparent, making it less likely for personnel departments of businesses or other funding sources to sponsor the work of trainers. Adding to the dilemma is the fact that omission of any of the four steps can result in ineffective or even counterproductive results.

Let us go back to the example presented at the beginning of the chapter. Mark and Susan have been exemplary members of the church and most likely take pride in the "good work" they have been doing for these "poor, helpless immigrants." Because at this point Mark and Susan are not aware of problems with their behaviors and attitudes, providing them with information about immigrant culture or showing them alternative ways of interacting is not likely to succeed. If trainers were to skip the *awareness* stage, their chances of success would be very unlikely.

Once awareness is established, the next step is to provide the trainees with appropriate *knowledge.* After going through awareness exercises and simulations, Mark and Susan should be much more conscious of how their past actions had been ethnocentric and culturally insensitive. This should then lead to a degree of embarrassment and a desire to learn more about culture and cultural differences. For example, trainers might want to focus on the point that the refugee community was noticeably perturbed by American volunteers abruptly terminating their visits after 6 months. In many cultures, the concept of volunteerism is nonexistent. To make sense out of this new experience, many refugees interpret the role of the volunteer as that of a friend and thus expect a long-term relationship from that person. As a result, when the volunteer moves on to another family after 6 months, the refugees often feel betrayed.

At this point trainers may feel inclined to plunge immediately into skills development. The danger, however, is that ethnocentrism is a way of thinking that is closely linked to people's sense of identity. The reason for this is that as children go through the process of socialization, life is simplified for them as being "good" or "bad." For example, most Anglo-American children are told that having their own *individual* opinions is "good," and that changing their opinions to please others is being "two-faced" and is, therefore, "bad." As these children grow into adulthood and interact in a culture such as that of the Japanese, who prize maintaining a clear distinction between *honne* (one's real intentions) and *tatemae* (one's social facade), several types of reactions often emerge. A common reaction is to evaluate the Japanese with the same concept of "good" or "bad," resulting in the conclusion that they are "bad" for being two-faced. A second reaction is confusion. Because children are brought up believing that everything is *either* good *or* bad, the concept that something could actually be both "good" *and* "bad" baffles many people, even as adults. The third possible reaction is to accept and adopt the other culture's standards of judgment and to deny one's own. In either case, cross-cultural interaction often brings to light many beliefs and assumptions about very basic aspects of life that would otherwise be left unchallenged, making it an extremely emotional experience for many. The *emotional challenges* brought on by extensive intercultural contact must therefore be addressed sufficiently during training.

The fourth and final stage, then, is *skills* acquisition. By now, Mark and Susan should be *aware* of how their past actions have been ethnocentric or culturally insensitive. They should also be much more *knowledgeable* about the immigrant culture and should have developed less ethnocentric attitudes. At this point they are much like people who have finally admitted the need to take swimming lessons, have learned the basic theory behind swimming, have overcome their fear of water, and yet have not practiced the actual arm and leg movements, not to mention having entered the swimming pool! Without actually learning how to swim, the previous steps would seem extremely wasteful. Unfortunately, as mentioned earlier, cross-cultural trainers constantly find themselves in a triple bind between: (a) limited time and budgetary constraints, (b) a lengthier process due to two additional steps (i.e., awareness and emotional challenges), and (c) steps that are sequential and that cannot be omitted. Trainers have approached this dilemma in a variety of ways. Kohls (1984), for example, advises against programs of less than 3 days and suggests 2 weeks if language training (e.g., some basic helpful phrases) is to be included. Others have found that they cannot afford this luxury and therefore use an incentive system where organizations are given large discounts similar to the "buy two, get one free" concept commonly found in supermarkets. Although trainers vary in their assessment of the minimum amount of time that is necessary for a good training program, we recommend that the four stages be followed through sequentially. Although the task may seem cumbersome, a good needs assessment may help trainers save time and make training more effective. For example, results of the needs assessment may reveal that trainees already have the *awareness* necessary to proceed directly into *knowledge*. In some cases, trainees may have the *awareness, knowledge,* and *emotional readiness* appropriate to proceed directly into *skills*.

The remainder of this chapter will briefly describe the stages of awareness posited by Sue et al. (1982) and will then proceed by describing the various dimensions of, as well as exercises that can be useful for, knowledge acquisition.

◆ **Awareness**

Sue et al. (1982) identified four awareness competencies and these were later expanded by Pedersen (1988). Although these were originally developed for counselors, they are general enough so that slight modifications should help expand their applicability.

SELF-AWARENESS

The first competency requires the trainees to move from being culturally unaware to becoming aware of the way their own lives have been shaped by the culture into which they were born. This should also be accompanied by learning to respect and be sensitive toward culturally different others.

CONSCIOUSNESS OF ONE'S VALUES AND BIASES
AND THEIR EFFECTS

The second competency requires conscious awareness of one's own values and biases and *how* they affect the way one interacts with culturally different people. Some values and biases cannot be changed or modified easily. Moreover, people may *not want* to change some of their values. However, being aware of their existence and their effect on their interactions with others can at least help trainees monitor their ethnocentrism. Although people do not like to think of themselves as being ethnocentric, it is only natural for them to view and to assess the outside world based on their own experiences. Since it follows that their experiences are largely influenced by the culture in which they live, ethnocentrism is often the result.

NECESSITY OF BECOMING COMFORTABLE
WITH DIFFERENCES

It is not possible nor is it healthy for people to adapt themselves to every value system in which they find themselves. People should not be afraid to recognize and admit that there are differences. In addition, they should feel comfortable with the awareness that they may not be able to behave according to these other values.

SENSITIVITY TO CIRCUMSTANCES

Being sensitive to circumstances implies that human beings are not infallible and that there may be certain cultural groups in which some people have a very hard time interacting. Instead of denying this difficulty, sometimes it is wiser simply to refer the client (or business partner or student) to someone else who is better able to serve the client. For example, certain counselors may note that they are having an unusually high failure rate with certain types of clients. The clients may be of a particular race or ethnicity or simply have certain traits that the counselors have trouble with, such as obesity. Although it is extremely important for the *counselors* to address those issues and attempt to resolve them for their own sakes, the *clients'* interests may be better served by a different counselor.

Pedersen (1988) describes in detail the various stages involved in developing multicultural awareness while introducing a wide variety of exercises trainers can use. Rather than making a haphazard attempt, in the limited space available, to describe some of the methods recommended for the various stages of awareness, we urge readers to refer directly to Pedersen's *A Handbook for Developing Multicultural Awareness*.

For the sake of illustration, however, one of the exercises will be described to show how awareness can be addressed in an actual training program. The "Outside Expert Awareness Exercise" (Pedersen, 1988, p. 28) can be used to help develop the first two awareness competencies and it can begin to address the other two. In this exercise approximately one third to one half of the training group are asked to be the "outside experts" assigned the task of entering a culture that is unknown to them and assessing as well as suggesting solutions for the problem(s) this culture has. The experts are instructed to interview members of the host culture individually to obtain information. The culture in question is made up of the rest of the training group, and in fact, has no specific problem. They do, however, have very distinct cultural characteristics that tend to cause a significant amount of stress and frustration on the part of the "outside experts." The three rules that this culture abides by are: (1) they can only answer "yes" or "no" questions; (2) men can only talk to men and women can only talk to women; (3) if the interviewer is smiling while asking a question, the interviewee must always answer "yes." If the interviewee is not smiling, the answer is "no" *regardless* of the content. The experts are given explicit instruction with regard to rule #1 but not the other two. As the "experts" interact with the "host population" many of their ineffective cultural assumptions come to the surface. A few that are especially significant are: speaking the same language ensures communication; the word *yes* should mean "yes"; the assigned task is always more important than establishing interpersonal relationships with the host culture; miscommunication is usually the result of a defect on the host culture population's part (i.e., they are deaf or they don't understand English well).

Through the use of simulations such as this, it is hoped that trainees learn to recognize the importance and urgency attached to learning more about culture and cultural differences, hence preparing them for the acquisition of knowledge.

◆ Knowledge

In this chapter "knowledge" will be divided into four general categories—immediate concerns, area-specific knowledge, culture-general knowledge, and culture-specific knowledge—in order to facilitate discussion.

Immediate Concerns. The first knowledge area trainers must address centers on issues that would otherwise distract trainees from fully involving themselves in the workshop. For example, when conducting training sessions for people immediately prior to their overseas assignments, questions regarding passports, school systems, housing, shopping, and churches tend to preoccupy their thoughts. Without addressing these issues first, trainers risk the chance of facing an extremely distracted audience (Rippert-Davila, 1985).

Area-Specific Knowledge. Specific knowledge regarding topics such as history, sociology, geography, politics, and economics helps trainees engage in intelligent conversations with people from the host culture. Americans going overseas, in particular, face an ongoing stereotype of the "ignorant American" who thinks that the national language of Switzerland is Swedish. In order to break this stereotype Americans need to make a special effort to be particularly knowledgeable about "area specific" content. Hosts appreciate trainees who have "done their homework" and who are informed about their culture.

Culture-General Knowledge. When cultures cross, regardless of the specific differences involved, certain common phenomena tend to occur. Anxiety, disconfirmed expectancies, and confrontation with one's prejudices are a few that will be discussed later in this chapter. These concepts tend to be widely applicable and can assist many types of trainees in their adaptation process.

Culture-Specific Knowledge. Culture-specific knowledge refers to customs, etiquettes, and rules that are specific to the various cultures. Although these include specific behaviors such as "an Islamic person's head is sacred and should not be touched," a laundry list of all possible "cultural rules" can be counterproductive due to its immensity. Rather than presenting specific behaviors, Brislin, Cushner, Cherrie, and Yong (1986) derived various themes that exhibit themselves repeatedly in cross-cultural interactions. By familiarizing themselves with the themes and using them to learn the specific cultural rules, trainees are then capable of "learning how to learn." This ability is repeatedly acclaimed as one of the most important skills trainees can acquire since once they leave the training facilities, they are, in fact, on their own (J. Bennett, 1986; Parker, Valley, & Geary, 1986; Trifonovitch, 1977).

◆ Immediate Concerns

Assume that program participants are foreign students beginning their sojourns in the United States. Certain issues such as housing, registration for classes, visa issues, health insurance, and shopping need to be addressed *before* delving into the complexities of the American culture. Otherwise, it is more than likely that trainers will face an extremely inattentive group. As Maslow's (1954) hierarchy suggests, unless basic human needs such as food, shelter, belongingness, and esteem are fulfilled, people are not psychologically prepared to seek further intellectual stimulation.

For other types of trainees such as social workers, health care workers, and counselors working within the United States, a different set of immediate issues may prevail. These may be doubts and concerns regarding the need to participate in a training session, or they may be questions or problems regarding current crises occurring at the workplace. The importance of addressing such issues cannot be overemphasized.

Not only are these excellent starting points for discussion, but adding relevance to the participants' work leads to increased attention and interest, as well as to a higher likelihood of skills transfer. One of the major dilemmas of any type of training, but especially for cross-cultural training, is that the training climate is so far removed from "real life" that many trainees experience difficulty applying concepts learned during training to their everyday lives. The use of actual problems experienced by trainees helps create a link between the training situation and the real world, increasing the possibility of the transfer of skills (Silberman, 1990).

There are several ways in which these issues may be addressed. One way is to provide the trainees with short readings prior to the first session. These materials should address some of the more common concerns participants in the past have expressed. For businesspeople with overseas assignments, for example, a checklist of things that need to be taken care of such as passports, visas, medical records (including vaccination information), insurance policies, school records, and international driver's licenses may be provided. Such lists can be found in Kohl's (1984) *Survival Kit For Overseas Living* and Harris and

Moran's (1979) *Managing Cultural Differences*. In addition, a panel discussion by "old hands" who are willing to share their experiences and answer questions can be an effective method of addressing immediate concerns. An extension of this method is to form a "big sister/big brother" system where trainees are assigned mentors they can turn to whenever help is needed, even after the training program ends. Although this is more commonly used for training personnel prior to their overseas assignments, this can be as effective for other types of cross-cultural training as well. For example, many social workers, counselors, or lawyers who find themselves working with a culturally different clientele may feel as though they lack a support system within their organizations or communities. Being able to meet "mentors," to hear their stories and to establish contact with them, can be golden opportunities for many people.

◆ Area-Specific Knowledge

According to a study conducted across nine countries, American students came in second to last in their knowledge of other cultures (Fantini, 1984). As mentioned earlier, the stereotype of the ignorant American is a persistent belief across the rest of the world. Due to this, it is often necessary for Americans to make a special effort to be especially knowledgeable about other peoples and cultures. If trainees are going abroad, being knowledgeable about local geography, economy, history, educational information, current events, and politics should facilitate interactions with the host nationals. For trainees interacting with ethnic minorities and other culturally different people within the United States, understanding their history, sociology, economics, psychology (Harper, 1973), geographic location, socioeconomic status, educational information, employment information, and family relationships (Henderson, 1979) is essential.

In addition to portraying a more intelligent self, the important nonverbal message sent through knowledge of these concepts is that the trainees *care* enough to spend numerous hours acquiring the knowledge. Because respect and trust are important prerequisites to establishing any sort of relationship (including business relationships) in many cultures, knowledge in this area can be extremely helpful in gaining acceptance into the group. Unfortunately, learning such information can be time consuming and tedious.

Often during a short cross-cultural training session, trainers opt to allocate time for raising awareness of the necessity of acquiring area-specific knowledge and then provide participants with a guided self-study reading list.

One method that is often used to raise awareness is a short quiz or inventory assessing trainee knowledge. One of the pitfalls shown by research, however, is that trainees who perform sufficiently well tend to be inspired to work harder while trainees who do poorly have a tendency to give up. In other words, the inventories result in discouraging those who need the knowledge most. Trainers, therefore, need to be careful when administering such material and to do so in a nonthreatening manner. Harris and Moran (1979, p. 528-535) and Kohls (1984, p. 86) have checklists of knowledge areas useful for trainees to know when going abroad. Presenting these as checklists of things to be learned rather than as a test of their knowledge is one approach trainers can use to alleviate the problem.

Given more time, however, several options are commonly used for the dissemination of area-specific knowledge. Surprising to some, perhaps, is the research that supports "straight lecturing" as being more effective than simulations in conveying *specific and unfamiliar* content knowledge (Brislin & Pedersen, 1976). Other methods that are often used are: group discussions, panel discussions among "old hands," audiovisual presentations, interviews with consultants and experts, observations, and library research. Parker, Valley, and Geary (1986) described the possibility of creating and presenting a Trivial Pursuit-type game as a means of gaining cultural knowledge about the four major ethnic groups represented in the United States.

◆ Culture-General Knowledge

Certain businesspeople may be sent to a specific country such as Japan for 5 to 6 years. Others, such as foreign student advisors, may find themselves interacting with people from a multitude of different cultures in any one given day. Although it would be ideal for them to know all the pertinent cultural rules of all the people they interact with, it is less than likely that they will have the time or perseverance to do so.

One alternative is to acquire *culture-general knowledge*. Such knowledge refers to specific theories or themes that are commonly encountered in cross-cultural interactions regardless of the cultures involved. Although these may not provide prescriptive behavior or concrete answers to one's dilemmas, they provide clues as to where the problem(s) may lie. This is similar to the list of symptoms doctors use to diagnose one's illness. Although the list does not enable the doctor to label the illness immediately, going down the list and checking off the relevant symptoms and crossing out the irrelevant ones narrows down the possibilities.

Because the aim of the rest of the chapter is to provide a workable framework with which to approach culture-general *as well as* culture-specific knowledge, we will utilize Brislin et al.'s (1986) 18 themes to form the basis of our discussion.

PEOPLE'S INTENSE FEELINGS

As mentioned earlier, cross-cultural encounters have a tendency to evoke intense feelings. The five themes found in this category are: (a) anxiety, (b) disconfirmed expectancies, (c) belonging, (d) ambiguity, and (e) confrontation with one's prejudices. Here is a critical incident that introduces these five themes as they might be experienced by an American sojourner in Japan.

Nancy, a Japanese American, was a junior at a prestigious private university on the East Coast. After studying Japanese intensively for the past 2 years, she applied and was chosen as one of the few students selected for the 1-year exchange program with a Japanese university. Nancy was extremely excited at the prospect of being able to "trace her roots" and was confident that she would do well in Japan. After several weeks at the university in Japan, however, she felt extremely discouraged and resentful toward the Japanese. Her confidence in her ability to speak the Japanese language diminished as soon as she arrived at the airport and realized that she could not understand anyone and no one could understand her. This came as an extreme shock for her since she had always excelled in all the Japanese classes she had taken *(disconfirmed expectancies)*. Due to this, Nancy felt extremely helpless, having constantly to depend on someone else for even the most basic necessities such as going shopping. She would also find people staring at her or laughing at her when she did things that would be considered normal in America *(anxiety)*. She gradually grew to be wary of interacting with the Japanese in general, since she never knew if she was doing the right thing or not *(ambiguity)*. Her identity was another problem for her. Having been one of the few Japanese Americans in her home town in the United States, Nancy thought of her journey to Japan as a chance to be with "her people." Much to her surprise, however, she received the "outsider treatment" from the Japanese since her language competency and gestures obviously defined her as a foreigner *(belonging)*. As weeks went by, Nancy decided she disliked everything Japanese *(prejudice)* and spent most of her time doing things with a group of American buddies she met at the university.

Anxiety. As adult sojourners find themselves in a country that is entirely new to them they are much like newborns. They know virtually nothing about social manners, language, or culture. Many find themselves at a loss with the transportation system, the supermarkets, and even the bathrooms! The all-important difference between adult sojourners and newborns is that the former have no one to take care of them. In fact, in many cases, they bring with them children whom *they* must care for.

The visual image we suggest is that of an American family of four who, after 12 hours of flying, an hour of going through customs inspection, and a 2-hour train ride, have finally arrived at Shinjuku station in Tokyo. The youngest child is crying due to hunger while the older one is desperate for a bathroom. The

parents cannot read the signs and are frantically looking for help but no one seems to speak English. . . .
    In Nancy's case, she has found that her normal, everyday behavior such as laughing out loud without covering her mouth is now evoking unwanted attention. She has also noticed that behaviors that have worked to her advantage in the United States, such as assertiveness, have produced adverse results for her in Japan. Needless to say, the anxiety level felt during the "normal, everyday life" of sojourners is much higher than that of people living in their country of birth.

Disconfirmed Expectancies. Often times, what is especially discouraging for many people is not necessarily the experience itself, but the disappointment that results from the gap between their expectations and the actual situations. For example, many of us would be disappointed if we went to see a "talking dog" and found that the dog did not speak. On the other hand, if we went to see our neighbor's dog, we would not be disappointed if it did not say anything because the *expectation* of its talking would have been nonexistent. This phenomenon presents interesting ramifications. It suggests that by lowering one's expectations to a realistic or even slightly pessimistic level, the amount of stress one encounters should decrease significantly. Nancy, for example, might not have felt as disappointed with her language competence or the fact that the Japanese were treating her as an outsider, if she had entered the country *expecting* those things to happen.

Belonging. Humans are by nature social beings. A look at Maslow's (1954) hierarchy reveals "belongingness" as coming third only to the need for food and shelter. It is suggested that what underlies this inherent need for acceptance and belonging are self-confirmation needs, and attention and emotional release needs, as well as esteem and security needs (Brislin et al., 1986). Groups, however, are defined to a large extent by their exclusionary functions. In other words, emphasizing the differences of the "outsiders" enhances the similarities of the "insiders"

(Gudykunst, 1986). The flip side of this otherwise functional mechanism is that those who are excluded from the group suffer a great deal of stress. Long-term sojourners who have made painstaking efforts to learn the language and culture of the host country in order to "fit in" are especially susceptible to this. This can provoke even more anxiety for people like Nancy, whose main purpose is to "trace their roots." For people like Nancy, being part of a minority affects their sense of belonging, provoking them to search for their parents' homeland. Much to their chagrin and shock, however, they realize that they again are outsiders in the other culture as well. In Nancy's case, this perhaps led her to strengthen her sense of affiliation with the American group at her university as they, in turn, excluded the Japanese from their group.

Ambiguity. As children are socialized into any given culture they learn what is appropriate, effective, appreciated, and revered as well what is not. Part of the stress that accompanies growing up stems from cultural rules that are learned through trial and error. As people reach adulthood, however, they reach a point of "cultural fluency" where they are able to function within those cultural parameters with relative effectiveness. If we use the analogy that cultural rules are the keyboard functions of a computer, adults of a society are computer literate people who are familiar with the functions of most of the keys. When these adults find themselves in an entirely new and different culture, however, they realize that the keys on the keyboard have been switched around. Life that used to be quite predictable becomes unpredictable and confusing. Tolerance for ambiguity has thus been cited in numerous cross-cultural studies as one of the most important characteristics for overseas success (Kealey & Ruben, 1983).

Confrontation With One's Prejudices. Although most people feel uncomfortable with the thought that they are prejudiced, many, in fact, are. This is because despite the multitude of negative connotations it contains, prejudice serves a number of purposes.

Two of the many functions it is said to serve are the utilitarian or adjustment function and the ego-defensive function (Katz, 1960).

As mentioned at the beginning of this chapter, cross-cultural encounters can be extremely stressful in that our beliefs of what is right or wrong are often challenged. When encountering people with differing beliefs it is much easier for people simply to dismiss them as being wrong or primitive rather than having to think carefully about them. For example, Ruben and Kealey's (1979) study showed that ethnocentric people tend to suffer less from culture shock since they are oblivious to the fact that their own system of beliefs may not necessarily be the best. Although these people were also shown to be less effective in the host culture, in terms of *adjustment* or mental stability, their ethnocentrism served the purpose of protecting their feelings of self-worth. Another function of prejudice is *ego-defensive*. Rather than admitting that a certain ethnic group is hardworking, industrious, or ingenious, it is much easier for people to label them as being cunning or scheming, thus taking the blame off oneself if the other group performs better on a number of important tasks.

BASES OF CULTURAL DIFFERENCES

A dog's bark is depicted by the onomatopoeia *ruff ruff* in English, *wan wan* in Japanese, and *gua gua* in certain parts of China. Given that people hear the same set of sounds emitted from dogs, the differences in the way the same stimulus is interpreted are attributed to the variance of commonly used phonemes in the languages. In the same way that the basic sounds differ across languages, it is also suggested that the basic frameworks used by people to organize and process other types of stimuli vary across cultures as well. Some of the large frameworks we use to make sense out of the environment are: (a) categorization, (b) differentiation, (c) the in-group/out-group distinction, (d) learning styles, and (e) attribution.

Categorization. According to Detweiler (1980, p. 277), categorization refers to "the way information is believed to be organized or grouped in meaningful ways in human memory." For example, when we are flipping through the yellow pages looking for a good place to buy roses, we find it conveniently listed under the category "florists." Without knowing the categories "florists" or "roses," identifying and buying roses would be an immense task. A quick exercise to prove this point would be to define a rose without using any categories. The task is virtually impossible. The Random House College Dictionary defines a rose as "any of the *wild* or *cultivated,* usually *prickly-stemmed, showy-flowered shrubs* of the *genus Rosa."* In order to understand this definition, at least nine other categories need to be understood. Thus categorization serves the purpose of simplifying and creating a sense of order in the environment. Certain types of facial expressions, for example, are classified as signifying approval, others disapproval. Certain actions are considered polite while others are rude. Because categories may vary across cultures, misunderstandings can occur as the same action is classified differently.

Another example of categorization is "stereotyping." Stereotypes are oversimplified generalizations made with regard to specific groups of people. For example, some typical stereotypes people hold are: the reserved British, the friendly but loud Americans, the emotional Italians, and the rigid Germans. When meeting someone for the first time, stereotypes provide people with a framework (accurate or not) from which to work. The problem with stereotypes is that many people use them to filter reality so much that the unique traits of the individuals they are interacting with are not appreciated. This can cause negative feelings as a result of the interaction due to the individuals' desire to be appreciated for their uniqueness.

Differentiation. Once information has been categorized, the subtleties must be looked at so that differentiating variables can be identified. For example, returning to the concept of buying a rose, once we have found what we identify as "roses" our next task is to choose which one to buy. In other words, one needs to examine the roses in order to determine which is fresher, more fragrant, has a nicer color, and so forth. In the same way, in the category "smiles," we need to distinguish those that portray happiness from simply polite or cunning facial expressions. In the category "greetings," we need to choose whether we will say "Hello!" or "Where are you going?"

Although differentiation itself is culture-general, the content and the criteria that are involved vary. For example, a smile that is interpreted by one culture as signifying happiness might be seen as cunning in another culture. Joking is appropriate in certain business settings in the United States but inappropriate in others. The very difficult task for the sojourner is learning the distinctions.

In-Group/Out-Group Distinction. As mentioned in the explanation for belonging, the formation of groups necessitates the existence of outsiders. By exaggerating the differences that outsiders have, the similarities of the group are further enhanced. A good example would be an exclusive country club where members have little, if anything, in common except wealth. What identifies them as members of the club is the exclusive privilege of using club facilities to which outsiders are not given access.

In the same way, the greatest source of unity for many countries is the existence of *other* countries. By defining the others as *different* from themselves, a stronger sense of unity among the members seems to develop. Many sojourners initially enjoy the differential treatment received while living abroad. At times, this treatment can be positive, as seen in the incident that introduced this chapter. After a few months or years of outsider treatment, however, anger and resentment toward host nationals often result.

Learning Styles. Although many countries have adapted the Western style of education that takes place in a classroom, some less urban, nontechnical societies use a more hands-on approach to education. Children are taught how to weave or to milk a cow by observing and practicing the motions with their elders. When placed in a classroom situation, many do not function well because the relevance of the materials is not as clear to their day-to-day lives. Even for the more urban technical societies where the basic Western school system is used, the styles of disseminating information vary. For example, many students from southeast Asia are significantly more comfortable with the professors as "speakers" and the students as "listeners." When these students come to the United States for their higher education, many are intimidated by the American teaching style where discussion is considered essential for effective learning.

Attribution. Imagine the following scene.

> You walk into a room where your friends are sitting and engaging in lively conversation. As you come closer to the group, however, they fall silent. Why do you think this happened?

Attributions refer to conclusions we make about the causes of people's behavior (Brislin et al., 1986). Upon reading the above scene, the most common interpretation was probably that they (the friends) were talking about you (the reader) before you came in. People make attributions constantly. As we greet co-workers in the morning, we observe how they look and make attributions regarding the type of mood they are in. Such attributions can be extremely helpful when trying to decide whether one should ask them for a favor or not. As people are enculturated into a society, they learn to make fairly accurate attributions about others' behaviors. Problems, however, arise in intercultural encounters where the same attributions should not necessarily accompany the same behaviors.

The Culture Assimilator is an effective way (Broaddus, 1986) to familiarize trainees with the 18 themes presented by Brislin and his colleagues (1986). By reading 100 critical incidents similar to the two anecdotes discussed earlier in the chapter and analyzing the themes that come into play, trainees should gain familiarity as well as competence with the application of the 18 themes. Although critical incidents are helpful in learning the themes, they tend to be far removed from the trainees' everyday life since they are incidents about *other* people. Having trainees write out critical incidents based on their experiences should help bridge the gap between the somewhat artificial training setting and their real lives. Even people who have little or no intercultural experience can analyze many of the themes by examining their interactions across other types of differences such as class, gender, and age.

◆ Culture-Specific Knowledge

The advantage of culture-general knowledge is that the concepts should be helpful regardless of the cultures involved. Although this can be extremely useful during the initial stages of adaptation, without knowledge of the specificities of the host nationals' culture, effective interaction is extremely difficult. The culture-specific knowledge themes should provide broad guidelines as to what exactly needs to be learned. The themes that fall in this category are: (a) work, (b) time and space, (c) language, (d) roles, (e) importance of the group and importance of the individual, (f) rituals and superstitions, (g) hierarchies: class and status, and (h) values.

WORK

When entering a new work setting many things are unclear and confusing. New employees are not yet aware of many norms such as how rigid the organization is in terms of work hours, how often employees socialize and its importance, how the "coffee club" operates, and who is *really* in charge.

Deal and Kennedy (1982) present five factors that determine corporate culture. The five are: (a) business environment, (b) values, (c) heroes, (d) the rites and rituals, and (e) the cultural network. Market factors such as types of products, competitors, customers, technologies, and government influences constitute the *business environment.* Because this largely affects whether emphasis is placed on selling, invention, or management of costs, it is said to be the single greatest influence in shaping a corporate culture (Deal & Kennedy, 1982).

Values, according to Deal and Kennedy's definition, are said to define success in concrete terms for employees while establishing standards for achievement within the organization. Successful companies are characterized by the prominence and the widespread agreement with regard to their values. These values make employees feel special by creating a sense of identity with the group. Often, catch phrases are created to serve as a reminder to the employees of the corporate values. Some examples are: "Quality at a good price" (Sears, Roebuck), "Better things for better living through chemistry" (DuPont), and "Strive for technical perfection" (Price, Waterhouse & Company) (Deal & Kennedy, 1982, p. 23). *Heroes* provide employees with a concrete ideal to strive for. They are people who illustrate corporate values through their extraordinary, yet possibly realistic, deeds. They, too, provide employees with a sense of unity if all can agree that certain people are indeed heroes.

Programmed routines of everyday life are referred to as *rites and rituals* (Deal & Kennedy, 1982). Rites and rituals sustain the corporate culture. They provide specific rules to follow such as how informally or formally people must be addressed, who speaks first in meetings, how prompt employees must be, and how they should dress. They also consist of more elaborate rituals such as ceremonies honoring outstanding employees, weekly breakfasts, and staff retreats.

A large portion of what goes on in an organization is independent of formal events and is affected by what is called the *cultural network* (Deal & Kennedy, 1982). The cultural network consists of the informal communication that takes place in organizations. Many times people take on specific roles, such as "storyteller" or "spy," that help them gain informal status symbols, such as the preferred office. Because the "cultural network" can sometimes command more employee trust and credibility than upper management does, effective use of it is essential (Brislin, 1991).

TIME AND SPACE

A common complaint heard from Americans visiting Mexico is that Mexicans are *not* punctual. Many Americans also note their discomfort as Mexicans stand *very* close to them during a conversation. Each culture has an unwritten but widely accepted set of rules regarding both time and space. In the United States, for example, promptness is highly prized. If a business appointment is made for 1:00 P.M., it is expected that the person will actually be there by that time. People make attributions regarding the person depending on how prompt or late that person is. For example, if people arrive half an hour early, the attribution will most likely be that they are terribly anxious. If they arrive 5 to 10 minutes early, they are reliable, and so on. Many of these rules are pounded into us during our socialization process such that deviation from these rules tends to provoke strong emotional reactions. For example, if someone is 3 hours late for an appointment, most Americans would be extremely angry, attribute it to irresponsibility, and most likely not seek further contact with that person.

Values regarding space tend to be equally emotional. For example, many American tourists label the Japanese as being rude for pushing and shoving in public. Many Mexicans feel that Americans are cool and detached because they insist on keeping a significant distance between themselves and others. Although intellectually understanding the cultural norms of other cultures is often not enough to emotionally accept their tardiness or their proximity, it is nonetheless a starting point.

LANGUAGE

Language is usually perceived as the single most important barrier to overcome when entering a new culture. As a result, most long-term training programs allocate a great deal of time and effort to language teaching. The problem with this approach, however, is the possibility of creating a "fluent fool." A fluent fool is someone who can speak a language fluently yet knows nothing about the culture. Since these people are fluent in the language, host nationals tend to assume that they must be equally fluent in the culture as well. A cultural misunderstanding, therefore, is less likely to be interpreted as due to the person's good-natured ignorance. On the other hand, people who do not speak the language well are often given the benefit of the doubt.

This does not imply that people should avoid language acquisition. Not attempting to learn the language is usually attributed to disinterest or condescension toward the host culture. The solution, therefore, is to integrate language training with culture learning. A good illustration of how language is intricately linked with culture can be seen in the translation of advertisements. This discussion assumes that trainers collect advertisements and provide translations of them. Because advertisements use a limited number of words to express a message, knowledge of the culture is *essential* to understanding them. For example, a Japanese advertisement for frozen breaded pork can be literally translated as "A *bento* [box lunch] that can be made with an oven toaster: Strong in the morning, delicious at noon." For the uninitiated observer of the Japanese culture, this advertisement probably makes little or no sense at all. To fully understand this advertisement it is necessary for people to know that the Japanese take fairly elaborate lunches to work, school, picnics, and other outings, and that it is important for the lunches to look as though plenty of time had been spent on them. Traditionally, women are expected to make *bentos* for their children, their husbands or, perhaps, for someone they love. If a woman is seen with an elaborate *bento,* many men interpret it as signifying that she will probably make a good wife. Although things are rapidly changing in Japan, and many working women do not have the time to make bentos, there is still some romantic significance attached to them. Two other factors that need to be understood is that most Japanese households do not have full-size ovens and that it is extremely time consuming and messy to make breaded pork from scratch. It is, therefore, a strong selling point to emphasize the fact that it can be made in an oven toaster in a matter of minutes. In addition, the phrase "strong in the morning" needs to be understood. The functional equivalent of the phrase in English would be "a morning person," suggesting that even women who are not "morning people" can appear as though they are with the help of this product.

ROLES

The teacher lectures while students listen and take notes. The father makes the rules that children must obey. Very often, our behaviors reflect the roles in which we find ourselves. For example, the role of an actress would justify the person who is pretending to be someone else. Without that role, the person would most likely be whisked into a mental institution. Expectations regarding roles vary across cultures. The function of a father as the disciplinarian, for example, does not apply in the Trobriand islands, where the maternal uncle is in charge of disciplining children (Malinowski, 1927).

Some of the role distinctions we find ourselves in are: roles within the family, sex roles, and work environment roles. Trainees can gain invaluable insight, as well as avoid unnecessary embarrassment, by interviewing local resource persons regarding the different expectations accompanying the various roles. Sexual harassment is often due to role misunderstandings. Men may adopt the role of "charming co-worker" and call positive attention to a woman's physical appearance. This may be an unwelcome aspect of a co-worker role from a woman's viewpoint.

IMPORTANCE OF THE GROUP
AND IMPORTANCE OF THE INDIVIDUAL

Individualism and collectivism have been two of the most extensively studied concepts in the field of intercultural communication (e.g., Bellah, Madsen, Sullivan, Swindler, & Tipton,

1985; Hofstede, 1980; Triandis, Bontempo et al., 1986; Triandis, Brislin, & Hui, 1988). The incident that introduced Chapter 1 included an analysis of individualism and collectivism. According to Hofstede's (1980) research, the United States is the world's most individualistic nation. In most American households, independence is perceived to be a positive characteristic. For example, it is not unusual for mothers to ask their 3-year-olds what they would like to drink. This serves as initial training for when the children leave their families at the age of 18 or so to go to college. Although some families support their children through college and possibly through graduate school, it is expected that once their children have entered the workforce they will be responsible for their own well- being. In fact, few people in the American culture *expect* to live with and be taken care of by their children in their old age.

In some cultures, however, choices are made for children by adults. Because adults are perceived to be wiser and more experienced, it is expected that they should know what is best for their children. By training children to accept the adults' (including their parents, aunts, uncles, and grandparents) decisions, they are being prepared for a lifelong relationship based on interdependence and loyalty. For example, it is not uncommon to find unmarried working men and women in Japan living with their parents. In some cultures, it is still the role of the parents to find marriage partners for their children. This, in return, means that in most of these cultures it is expected that the children live with and take care of their parents in their old age.

The relative importance placed on the individual and the collective obviously influences the way people interact. Reggie Smith, who had played on a Japanese baseball team for awhile, illustrated the frustrations of an individualist functioning in a collectivist society when he said:

> Major leaguers are self-assertive and aggressive, perhaps too aggressive for the Japanese, yet they develop their own individual styles and find something that works for them and stick with it.

The attitude the Japanese coaches (especially the Giants coaches) take toward their younger players is, "You're dumb. You don't know anything about baseball. Don't think. I'll tell you everything you need to know."... There is very little anticipation on the part of the players during games. They just wait to be told what to do . . . (Whiting, 1989, p. 320)

Beliefs regarding the importance of the individual and importance of the group, again, tend to be highly emotional. Understanding the reasons behind people's behaviors often does not correspond with emotional acceptance of their actions. Nonetheless, being aware of the extent to which people seem to value one or the other should help facilitate understanding of their behaviors (see Chapter 4, pp. 93-95, for more about individualism and collectivism).

RITUALS AND SUPERSTITIONS

Rituals range from day-to-day behaviors such as greetings to more commemorative ones that mark special occasions. Some are widely accepted within a single culture while some vary according to individual idiosyncrasies. The ritual of shaking hands when meeting someone for the first time, for example, is widely accepted in the United States. The ritual of eating green M & Ms before the other ones, however, may be just as important to a certain individual, yet is by no means widely accepted.

Rituals create a sense of order in an otherwise chaotic world. Adherence to rituals, therefore, provides people with a comfortable sense of predictability. When rituals are not followed, confusion sets in. For example, if two people are meeting for the first time and the first person puts out his hand while the second person simply stares at it, confusion and tension are likely to mount. Rituals are often linked to the various roles in which people find themselves. For example, Frank, an American, may find himself going through the ritual of kissing his wife good-bye in the mornings (husband), driving his children to their schools (father), having coffee with his co-workers (worker), going to church services on Sundays (Christian), and so forth. Superstitions, contrary to popular belief, exist all over the world in varying frequency. Although Americans like to consider themselves as rational people, certain superstitions are still pervasive. The superstition of "Friday the 13th" does not unduly worry most Americans. An example of this superstition coming to light, however, was seen in the mid-1980s when American passengers were reluctant to fly on Boeing's DC-10, which was making its first "recovery flight" on Friday the 13th, after its planes had been grounded for a period of time due to numerous accidents. A related phenomenon is the fact that few hotels in the United States refer to a 13th floor.

Some cultures have more superstitions than others. For many people, superstitions have a sacred quality to them. Although they may not be able to explain the superstition rationally, its importance remains uncontested. If a superstition is broken and something negative happens to occur that day, it is only natural for believers to blame it on the superstition. Sojourners should, therefore, be extremely careful with superstitions. No matter how *irrational* they may seem to the sojourner, their relevance to the host nationals should be enough justification to support it.

For example, one of the critical incidents presented by Brislin and colleagues (1986) describes a U.S. branch of a Japanese manufacturing plant where various traumas hit many of the workers within a period of a few months. Besides a rash of accidents within the plant itself, a car accident and the death of an executive's child followed. Rumors spread until the employees were convinced that the plant was jinxed and that a Shinto priest must be brought in to bless the plant. Given this scenario many American executives would rather reinforce safety and quality control within the plant. Without the Shinto priest's blessings, however, the employees will most probably continue to suffer from the curse because they believe in it. Respecting the employees' needs and providing them with appropriate measures will most likely increase productivity and efficiency rather than provoke further tension. If the managers were to disregard the employees' needs and some other accident were to occur, employee morale and trust in upper management would plummet. When interacting with culturally different others, people need to be especially sensitive to the rituals and superstitions the others may have.

HIERARCHIES: CLASS AND STATUS

Hierarchies exist in every culture. What differs when examining societies cross-culturally is that the level of hierarchy, the manner in which it is shown, and its desirability vary. For example, in the United States the belief that "all people are equal" prevails. Subordinates often call their bosses by their first names to show that they are in fact equal. The hierarchy nonetheless exists in that the bosses most likely receive a significantly higher salary, live in a larger house, and would still expect a certain degree of deference from their subordinates. Although hierarchies do exist in the United States, it is considered appropriate *not* to accentuate this fact.

In sharp contrast lies the Filipino culture, which according to Hofstede's (1980) study ranks extremely high in power distance. In other words, people are required to verbalize their hierarchical differences clearly and to recognize them as appropriate. Attitudinal differences with regard to hierarchies can cause difficulty when interacting with culturally different others. A classic case is that of a Filipina nurse in the United States who is told by her doctor to give a patient a certain type of medication. Even though the nurse is aware that the doctor has prescribed the wrong medication and that it will cause adverse reactions in the patient, she feels compelled to follow the doctor's orders without disputing him. American doctors would be shocked by this behavior because nurses in the United States are expected to ask questions if they have doubts about a doctor's orders.

Another example of a cross-cultural dilemma arising from differing perceptions of hierarchy occurs when Americans go abroad. Because most Americans believe that acknowledging a hierarchy violates their civil rights, many insist on bringing in the "call me by my first name" attitude to the work setting. In cultures such as Japan, where hierarchies determine everything from how a person must be addressed to the type of language that must be used, the American attitude is perceived as showing disrespect.

VALUES

According to Rokeach (1979), "values are core conceptions of the desirable within every individual and society. They serve as standards or criteria to guide not only action but also judgment, choice, attitude, evaluation, argument, exhortation, rationalization and one might add attribution of causality" (p. 2). Values create an element of order and rationality within a society. The problem again arises when people cross cultural boundaries. What is perceived as good or correct in one culture is seen as bad or incorrect in another.

Because values lie at the core of many of the previously discussed themes, understanding them should prove useful. One way to find out what the prominent values of a culture are is by collecting a list of sayings, quotes, proverbs, or fables. These generally provide a good range of the types of values that are considered important within the culture (Kohls, 1984). Because there should be an abundance of sayings, with some being more prominent than others, making use of a cultural informant should be considered. Cultural informants can help pick out the more relevant sayings and explain their significance within their culture. At times, sharp contrasts will become evident. For example, the Japanese saying "the nail that sticks up will get hammered down" is the approximate reverse of the American saying "the squeaky wheel gets the grease."

For culture-specific knowledge, the most effective approach is for trainees to "learn how to learn" because the amount as well as the types of knowledge needed will not only be immense, but will change over time. Once trainees have familiarized themselves with the various themes through critical incidents, their next task is to gather specific information relevant to them. Kohls (1984, p. 88) and Althen (1984, pp. 157-166) provide lists of questions and activities that should help trainees "learn how to learn." Trainees should also be encouraged to formulate a list of questions based on the eight themes that can guide the acquisition of culture-specific knowledge. These questions trigger further learning about the host culture and allow trainees to portray genuine interest. Some questions that may be helpful are:

1. If you were invited to a dinner party that started at 6:00 P.M., what time would you generally show up? (Time)
2. What time do most people get to work and what time do they leave? (Work & Time)
3. If your children were misbehaving, who would be in charge of disciplining them? (Role)
4. If you went out to a restaurant with a group of friends, would you split the cost evenly, would one person take the tab, or would you pay only for what you have eaten? (Individualism and Collectivism)

Although some cultural aspects are better revealed through direct questioning, others are better understood through observation. Another approach, therefore, is for trainees to "shadow" a few different people within the culture. For example, a social worker who is assigned to a largely Ukrainian community may want to "shadow," or follow around, a few Ukrainians from the community on several different occasions. In addition, shadowing a more experienced social worker for a day or two should provide a different set of insights. During this process, trainees should carry the list of the eight culture-specific themes and make a point of jotting down significant observations they have made.

◆ Conclusion

Awareness and knowledge are necessary first steps in a good intercultural communication training program. Very often, dealing with differences in knowledge brings on emotional

reactions among trainees. Nancy, for example, who was introduced earlier in this chapter, experienced strong feelings such as
anger, resentment, and dislike toward the Japanese. The discussion of her experiences revealed that the main reasons for these
feelings could be attributed to: (a) her lack of knowledge with
regard to cross-cultural adjustment, as well as, (b) the differences in the *types* of cultural knowledge she held, given her
socialization in the United States. Even though she was faced with
differences that can be analyzed in terms of knowledge, there
is no denying the emotional intensity of her reactions. Chapter 3
discusses the emotional impact of intercultural encounters and
also introduces one of the most memorable and intense aspects
that result from these encounters: culture shock.

3

Emotional Challenges

◆ The Spouse

Karen is the spouse of the branch president of a large multinational corporation in Mexico. Karen, her husband Jerry, and their two children moved to Mexico from Colorado 4 months ago. This is Jerry's first overseas assignment and marks a significant step up his career ladder. For Karen, the first few weeks in Mexico were filled with excitement and stimulation. Lately, however, she has found herself in bouts of depression and has contemplated suicide. After talking to a friend back in California, Karen has decided to seek professional help.

C (Counselor): Karen, would you like to tell me a little bit more about what's bothering you?

K (Karen): Well . . . nothing really . . . actually . . . everything! I feel tired and stressed out all the time even though I'm not really doing much! I don't work, we've got maids to do the cooking and the cleaning, and our driver takes the kids to school, so there's no reason for me to be unhappy. But I am . . . I feel as though I'm wasting my life away . . .

C: I understand you had a pretty challenging job back in California . . .

K: Yeah, I did . . . it wasn't all fun and games, you know . . . but at least I felt like I was doing something with my life. Now I feel as though I'm letting life pass me by and I can't do anything about it!

C: You're feeling sort of trapped . . .

K: Yeah, with the kids here and everything I can't just go home you know . . . And I'm so far away from my friends and family . . . I've met some nice people here but it's not the same . . .

C: The distance . . . it's making you feel really isolated . . .

K: Definitely . . . and helpless, too . . . I can't even ask directions without one of my children there to interpret for me! It's so frustrating because I feel so dependent on them! I feel as though I've lost authority over them. I can't even help them with their homework if it's in Spanish!

C: And that definitely adds to your sense of helplessness then . . . not only are you off your career track but you feel as though you're failing your job as a mother as well . . .

K: I feel so useless . . .

◆ Stress and Life Overseas

Living abroad can be extremely stressful for many people. Unfortunately, it is very difficult to document the result of such stress. Traditionally, the figures used as evidence for the stressful nature of overseas assignments have been the percentage of premature returns. According to Copeland and Griggs (1985), it is estimated that approximately 20%-50% of people sent on international business assignments return home prematurely. It has also been estimated that those sent to developing nations have an even higher early attrition rate of 70%. Although these findings combined with the documentation of the cost involved per family returning prematurely ($50,000 to $200,000, Harris & Moran, 1987) are convincing bottom-line figures, they reflect crisis situations and by no means represent the overall percentage of people experiencing levels of stress much higher than what they would normally encounter in their home countries. In other words, it is more than likely that a large percentage of people who have "successfully" completed their overseas assignments have endured large amounts of stress as well.

As suggested by the opening case study as well as the People's Intense Feelings themes presented in Chapter 2, some of the more emotional issues often relate to isolation, disorientation, general anxiety, disconfirmed expectancies, belonging, ambiguity, and confrontation with one's prejudices. The case study also introduces some problems faced by spouses who follow their husbands or wives to a foreign country. Although more attention has been given recently to spouses and families, in the past many organizations provided cross-cultural training *exclusively* to their employees. Unlike businesspeople who are assigned to specific tasks in a given country, accompanying spouses often have no clear role to fulfill there. In the past, the majority of these were women. In some cases, spouses had no real interest in going abroad or were extremely hesitant about doing so. Besides coping with their own adjustment problems, these women were given the additional tasks of providing comfort for their husbands and children who were undergoing culture shock, maintaining an orderly household using unfamiliar products, and being the upper level executive's wife. Because most of these assignments involved a significant promotion for the businessmen, many of the spouses found themselves as the upper level executive's wife for the first time in their lives. For many of these women, learning to host numerous cocktail parties, managing household help, and coping with their husbands' frequent business trips posed unexpected challenges (Shibusawa & Norton, 1989).

Another factor contributing to the stress level experienced by spouses is the lack of understanding they receive from other people. Many spouses, especially those who are sent to developing nations, are often provided with housekeepers, chauffeurs, and memberships in exclusive country clubs, as well as special travel privileges. This elevation in status makes them a target of envy of both host nationals and friends and family back home, furthering their sense of isolation. Spouses thus have few, if any, people to whom they can disclose their problems. For women who have given up their own careers to accompany their husbands, an additional dilemma of adjusting from "Hi! I'm so and so and I do such and such" to "Hi! I'm so and so's wife" adds to their identity crisis (Shibusawa & Norton, 1989).

Thus far this discussion has centered on spouses of upper level managers who are too often regarded as being "problem-free," leading the lives of aristocrats, playing golf every day, and traveling all over the world. A closer look, however, has revealed a myriad of stressors that plague their lives. Other types of sojourners, such as businesspeople, their children, immigrants and their families, and foreign students and their families, also encounter various stress-related problems. The rest of the chapter will cover the types of emotional challenges that are involved when people are placed in unfamiliar cultures, and a discussion of stress and stress management as they pertain to cross-cultural training.

◆ Milton Bennett's Developmental Model

Milton Bennett (1986) provides a model that describes the various stages people go through when placed in an unfamiliar culture. His model describes what happens in people's minds when thrust into a new and completely foreign culture where they must function according to rules that are virtually incomprehensible to outsiders. M. Bennett presents six stages: (1) denial, (2) defense, (3) minimization, (4) acceptance, (5) adaptation, and (6) integration. He labels the first three stages (i.e., denial, defense, and minimization) the "ethnocentric stages" and the next three stages (i.e., acceptance, adaptation, and integration) the "ethnorelative stages."

DENIAL

People who have lived most of their lives in a relatively homogeneous community tend to be in this stage. Because these people have had little, if any, contact with culturally different others, it is undoubtedly difficult for them to conceptualize the possibility that others may operate on a completely different value system from themselves. Further, they cannot entertain the thought that what they believe is "right" may not necessarily be so for others. When these people see differences, they do not attribute them to culture. Instead, they usually make an immediate value judgment. For example, instead of thinking that "the Filipinos place a high value on human interactions," they are likely to think that "the Filipinos are lazy, they socialize all the time, and they don't do any work." In other words, they impose their own value system of what is good or bad on other people. Unless everything is done their way it is "bad." A typical behavior of people in this stage, therefore, is to "enlighten the locals" by teaching and imposing their way of doing things. They also tend to talk louder and slower when they feel that the locals do not understand!

DEFENSE

During defense, people begin to recognize that their value systems may not be absolute. Often, they feel threatened by this thought and, as a result, cast negative stereotypes onto others. Although one may wonder why people should feel threatened, it is understandable when we consider how our self-concepts tend to rely heavily on the way we perceive ourselves with regard to our cultural values. For example, Americans who work hard, make a respectable salary, and have leisure time for hobbies most likely perceive themselves as successes. Their self-esteem and self-confidence probably rest largely on the hard work that led to achievement of this American value. Now, if they were to enter a different culture where the same value is seen differently, their basis of self-esteem and their lifelong effort at achieving this particular goal would be undermined. Comments such as "the Japanese work too hard, they don't know how to enjoy life," or "the Mexicans are just lazy," are typical efforts at defending their own values. In other words, people in this stage are more or less conscious of the fact that other value systems may exist. However, because they are afraid to acknowledge that fact because of its ramifications for their self-esteem, they resort to defensive behaviors such as negative stereotyping of others.

MINIMIZATION

A characteristic of people in this stage is to admit that although there are differences between cultures, they are insignificant compared to the similarities human beings, in general, have. A former project director of preservice training for Peace Corps volunteers in the Philippines told the following story.

> One of my training groups consisted of experienced teachers from the United States. I guess their average age was around 30. The problem broke out when I told them that as part of their training program they were to student-teach for 8 weeks. They got very angry with me, telling me that it was a waste of their time . . . they were experienced teachers and were here to "train the local teachers on the most modern teaching methodologies." They didn't understand why it was important for them to first observe how classes operated in the Philippines and the types of teaching methodologies that appeal most to the Filipinos . . .

The assumption behind the volunteers' reactions was that "teaching is universal," that what works in the United States should also work in the Philippines. Ironically, they insisted that a better use of their time would be to learn about the Filipino culture! Perhaps a common tendency for people in the minimization stage is to be unaware that culture is an integral part of everything, shaping even the most basic aspects of our lives, such as preferred teaching styles and the organization of schools. These volunteers were aware that differences existed but naively perceived them to be on a more superficial level such as the types of food eaten, dress, preferred forms of music and entertainment, as well as other cultural phenomena that are clearly visible. The general attitude taken by people in the minimization stage is that beneath superficial differences, humans beings are basically the same. Although this statement may be true to a certain degree, its usefulness for understanding other cultures is limited.

For example, it is valid to assume that children are at school to learn. It may not be valid to assume that using the American style of teaching, which tends to be more interactive and student-oriented, will work in the provinces in the Philippines. This is because the interactive form of learning is based on the American value of egalitarianism, which is not as predominant in the Philippines. On the contrary, according to Hofstede (1980), the Philippines rank very high in power distance, meaning that authority and hierarchy are given utmost respect and credence. Teachers sharing their authority with students through student-led discussions and other forms of interactive learning would not be seen as open-minded. Rather, the teachers would most likely be perceived as lazy and incompetent. Trainees in this stage need to learn that culture is much deeper than visible superficial differences and that pure and simple good intentions may actually lead to misunderstandings and conflict.

ACCEPTANCE

Acceptance marks entry into ethnorelativism. At this point, people have finally accepted that their values and norms are not necessarily "right" and that other cultures have their own values and norms that are just as respectable. Differences, no longer judged in terms of "good or bad," are accepted and respected as "facts of life." The following is a statement from someone who has found herself in this stage (this statement, and two others later in this chapter, are from people we have interviewed).

I know that Ukrainians don't view time as rigidly as I do, but when they keep me at their house for hours drinking coffee and eating, I can't help but worry about the time I am wasting.

The fact that she does not cast any value judgments on her Ukrainian friends reveals that she is not ethnocentric. However, the fact that she is still experiencing strong feelings of conflict with regard to the value clash between her and her friends shows that she still needs to adapt and to develop behavioral strategies to overcome this dilemma.

ADAPTATION

Adaptation is marked by behavioral changes. People not only accept cultural differences but are able to empathize with individuals from other cultures and change their behaviors when interacting with them. This does not mean that people must lose their cultural identity. Rather, this implies that they have become bicultural or multicultural. For example, this may mean being prompt with Americans while not placing such a premium on punctuality with Mexicans. This may mean switching from being extremely agreeable with the Japanese to engaging in animated debates with Germans. Although this may mean drastic changes in one's behaviors (to be discussed at greater length in the next chapter), we must remember that the key concept here is empathy. Once people are truly able to empathize with people from other cultures, these behaviors should come naturally and not feel artificial. Becoming bicultural or multicultural is not easy. It can be especially difficult for Americans, who believe that people should have one consistent personality and that changing one's behaviors to please others is not being true to oneself. The following quotation illustrates the fears and concerns of a person who has recently realized that she has become bicultural.

> I first realized that I was bicultural when I was walking around with my friend John and we bumped into my Japanese friend Miyako and her family. After Miyako and her parents walked off, John commented on how differently I acted when I was with them (the Japanese). He mentioned that I bowed a lot, my voice was higher, and that I curled my shoulders in when I talked. I was really shocked, because I was doing it unconsciously. After that I started paying more attention to "my two personalities." I realized that my Japanese friends described me as the type that would make a good "mother," while my American friends were telling me that I was definitely the "career type" and that they could not imagine me being married! This confused me. I wondered if I had a split personality or something . . .

People in the adaptation stage characteristically possess the behavioral skills to be effective in more than one culture. What distinguishes them from those in the following stage is that they have not yet integrated their biculturalism or multiculturalism into their identities.

INTEGRATION

A continuation of the preceding quotation illustrates this same person's move from adaptation to integration.

Now I am conscious of how differently I act with the two groups and no longer feel guilty about it. I know that my core personality is the same; I just act differently so I can function better in the two societies. I also realized that my friends' comments were not based on *facts* but were simply based on *their perceptions* of me and that I was in fact the same person. My friends from both cultures were simply telling me that I was behaving "favorably" within that culture. Now that I understand that there is nothing wrong with this "incongruence," I feel much more comfortable making the conscious switch from one culture to another.

Moving into this stage obviously involves much introspection. People must learn to integrate multiple sets of values into their identities even when some of the values may clash with one another. This is much more difficult than it may appear. Individuals who find themselves between two cultures are often treated as advocates or foes by both sides. For example, Americans who speak fluent Spanish and are equally as proficient with the Mexican culture as they are with the American culture are likely to be treated as "Mexico experts" by Americans and "U.S.A. experts" by Mexicans. At the same time, if these people seem too sympathetic toward the Mexicans, they are likely to be regarded as outcasts by Americans. Similarly, if they seem too sympathetic to Americans, they are likely to be dismissed as "yet another bunch of gringos" by the Mexicans. On good days these people feel as though they belong to two cultures, while on bad days they feel as though they are outcasts of both cultures. Although the importance of such people in an increasingly internationalizing world cannot be overestimated, the fact that becoming bicultural or multicultural is not "a bed or roses" needs to be understood as well. A good way to understand the integration stage is by looking at Third Culture Kids (TCKs). In today's world where joint ventures increasingly occur across national border lines, products are no longer made in one single country. Cars, for example, are no longer "made in Japan" but are usually made up of parts from all over the world and are then assembled in a country that is strategically placed for the company. A by-product of internationalization that is often overlooked are children who are born and raised overseas. Useem (1973) introduced the term *Third Culture Kids* to describe people who are now or once were dependents of adults with extended overseas job assignments. These adults have typically been missionaries, businesspeople, students, foreign service personnel, military personnel, technical and educational mission representatives, foreign correspondents, Peace Corps volunteers, artists, musicians, or teachers. TCKs are often exposed to their parents' cultures at their homes and the host-country culture outside of their homes. In addition, many TCKs who attend "international schools" or "American schools" are often exposed to a mixture of different cultures simultaneously. TCKs often do not feel completely at home with any one culture. The culture they are most familiar with is a "third culture," one that exists in the interstices of several cultures. For example, Korean TCKs who have spent most of their lives in the United States may feel uncomfortable identifying themselves as being either Korean or American. The culture they identify with is more likely a combination of the two cultures. Although this "third culture" may not be widely recognized by the general public, it is nonetheless a reality for many TCKs.

Many TCKs are bicultural or multicultural, fitting into Bennett's adaptation stage. A problem that often confronts many TCKs, however, is the need to integrate this into their identities once they return home. Because TCKs living abroad often find themselves in a unique environment where biculturalism or multiculturalism is a common phenomenon, they often do not find the need to integrate it into their identities. Most of the people they interact with are also TCKs and therefore do not question each others' existence. When TCKs return home, or in some cases move to their parents' homeland for the first time in their lives, they are confronted by a multitude of questions that challenge their identities. A simple question such as "Where are you from?" can trigger conflicting feelings within TCKs, because many people will persistently pursue the question with "Well . . . which culture do you feel most familiar with?" or "Which country do you like better?" People often pursue the question until they have forced the TCK to choose one country. As TCKs act as cultural mediators between different cultures, they are often torn between their dedication toward both cultures. Living in a world where the majority of individuals are still monocultural and cannot fathom the idea that people can be a combination of two or more cultures, TCKs must not only make an effort to integrate their "TCK-ness" into their identities but must also learn to be comfortable having their identities constantly challenged.

◆ The Bennett Model and Training Strategies

If trainers familiarize themselves with the Bennett model, they can assess which stage trainees are in and utilize methods most appropriate for different trainees. Without understanding this, trainers can make one of two mistakes. One is to use methods that are too basic for the participants, and the other is to assign techniques that are designed for people in the more advanced stages of cultural sensitivity. An example of the former would be assigning a basic cultural awareness exercise to trainees who are already in the acceptance stage and ready and willing to learn behavioral strategies to complement their awareness and understanding of cultural differences. These trainees are likely to be bored by the program and will likely lose interest and enthusiasm. An example of the latter would be to assign an exercise designed for people in the adaptation stage, such as complete cultural immersion experiences (below, and Chapter 5), to a group of trainees who are in the denial stage. This could result in a variety of possible outcomes. If the experience is unpleasant, trainees are likely to develop strong negative stereotypes about the people with whom they are interacting. If the experience is pleasant, cultural differences may go unnoticed, and thus trainees will reaffirm their beliefs that people everywhere are the same. Yet another possible outcome is for people to be scared off by the experience and avoid further interaction with culturally different others.

The key, then, is to be as helpful as possible to each training group by accurately assessing which stage trainees are in and providing appropriate activities to suit their levels of cultural sensitivity. For trainees in the denial stage, Bennett suggests non-threatening awareness activities such as "Tahiti Night" where people gather to eat and drink Tahitian food, listen to their indigenous music, see slide shows, and watch traditional dances. Other alternatives suggested are travelogues, history lectures, and examinations of ethnic literatures. The goal is to place trainees in a comfortable environment where they can start to recognize that differences exist. For trainees in the defense stage, it is suggested that commonalties, especially those that are considered as "generally good" in all cultures, be emphasized. For example, trainers can lead a discussion on what is "good" about the American culture as well as the "good" aspects of the host culture. According to Bennett, it is premature to try to convince defensive trainees that culture is neither good nor bad because making value judgments is inevitable for people in this stage. Trifonovitch[1] (1977), however, utilizes a more interactive approach with trainees in this stage who find themselves attaching strong negative stereotypes onto people of other cultures. Abiding by the principle that culture is more effectively learned on the affective level rather than the cognitive level (Aronson, 1972), Trifonovitch used the following method to erase the stereotypes that his Peace Corps volunteers had about "lazy Pacific Islanders." During his training programs, he assigned one day as "Micronesia Day." Naive trainees were excited with the prospect of spending a leisurely day "Micronesian style" until they woke up to find that there was no electricity, running water, or food. Their breakfast consisted mainly of coconuts that the Micronesian staff collected and cracked open. The rest of the day was spent gathering and preparing food Micronesian-style. After spending a whole day slaving about for food and not getting enough to eat, the volunteers learned to empathize more with Pacific Islanders. Trifonovitch admitted, however, that some defensive trainees reacted in a very hostile manner toward the training program and that some staff became "burned out" dealing with angry trainees.

For trainees in the minimization stage, Bennett suggests inviting "representatives" of other cultures as resource persons. Because people in this stage believe that cultural differences are only superficial, another strategy may be to invite experienced sojourners who can attest to the fact that cultural differences are much deeper. Once these people have been carefully chosen, they may be asked to participate in a panel discussion followed by questions and answers. Another possibility is to break into small groups, each with one resource person. The primary aim is for trainees to recognize that there may be more to cultural differences than meets the eye. In either case, trainers must be careful to select people who are culturally aware themselves. One dangerous assumption some trainers make is that being a minority, a foreigner, or having previous overseas experience excludes people from being ethnocentric. This is a myth, and trainers need to be aware of the dangers of inviting ethnocentric resource people.

Trainees who are in the acceptance stage have finally entered the realm of ethnorelativism. They recognize cultural differences and no longer need to make value judgments constantly. Now they need to develop behavioral strategies that make them more effective in intercultural situations. Trifonovitch (1977) used the strategy of exposing his trainees to situations where some of their more important values were violated. For example, he would arrange to have a meeting at a specific time but have the staff arrive 30-45 minutes later. Another strategy he took was deliberately extending their meetings far beyond the allotted time. Yet another strategy was to bring a live pig to the training site because he knew Americans would treat the pig as a pet. At the end of their orientation program, he would have the trainees kill and eat the pig for their last dinner. His aim in doing this was to have trainees experience how it feels to have some of their more important values violated and also for them to accept and adopt strategies to deal with these cultural differences. Another strategy used by Trifonovitch was to have nightly entertainment Micronesian-style where people would take turns performing for the benefit of others. American participants would be coaxed into performing, thus acquiring the ability to entertain others, a very important skill to have in Micronesia.

Finally, people in the adaptation stage need to learn how to integrate cultural relativity into their identities. They may become bicultural or multicultural, able to switch from one culture to another easily and skillfully. The developmental task that awaits trainees in this stage is to integrate this into their identity. Discussions of the difficulties bicultural and multicultural people face as minorities in a monocultural world should be helpful. In addition, inviting a panel of people who comfortably find themselves in the integration stage, and are willing to share their past as well as ongoing conflicts, should prove to be effective as well. The goal is for trainees to recognize that being adept in more than one culture is not only a useful skill but is one that requires significant adjustments within their identities.

◆ **Some Final Comments on the Bennett Model**

Although the Bennett model appears to be sequential in nature, like all models it is not absolute. For example, some people may not start at the denial stage. Others may not necessarily go through the whole continuum of stages but may stop at one point. Some people may skip over certain stages, while others may regress to an earlier one. Some people may even find themselves in a mixture of various stages. This, however, does not negate the relevance of this model but merely reaffirms that there are individual differences in how people adjust to another culture. Models are simplified conceptualizations of complex human behavior and must therefore be treated as such.

Bennett does, however, acknowledge that certain subcultures that have been oppressed by a dominant culture (i.e., Blacks, Hispanics, and Native Americans in the United States) seem to go through these stages in a different manner. He argues (Bennett, 1991) that when looking at the three ethnocentric stages (denial, defense, and minimization), oppressed minorities tend to skip over the first and the third and instead spend a considerable amount of time in defense. His reasoning is that oppressed minorities are often in situations where they see and feel differences between themselves and the dominant group. Therefore, denial or minimization of differences is less likely to occur in their minds. Instead, defending their own cultural identities through negative stereotyping of others' is more likely to occur since, as a repressed group, the need to solidify their identities has historically been extremely strong.

Bicultural people who are members of a minority group must also be given special consideration. An example would be people who speak standard English and act in a typical white middle-class manner when socializing with people outside of their ethnic group but who can switch to their "neighborhood" talk and act in a socially accepted manner within their own ethnic group as well. According to the Bennett model, these people would most likely fall in either the adaptation or the integration stage. The question, however, is what happens when these people are thrust into a completely new and different culture (e.g., as part of an overseas assignment). Are they more likely to skip over the ethnocentric stages because they are already bicultural, or are they more likely to start at stage one once again? These are intriguing questions that need further research and exploration. At this point, however, trainers should keep in mind the possibility that minority members, especially bicultural minority members, are likely to develop intercultural sensitivity in a different manner from the dominant group in any one country.

◆ Anxiety, Stress, and Stress Reduction

After 5 months in Honduras, Mike is pleased with the way things have been going for him at work. His position as the branch president is a clear step up his career ladder, and although he had initial problems understanding how to relate to Hondurans, he now has close relationships with many of his local workers and co-workers. Unfortunately, however, he has not felt very good physically. He has been having trouble sleeping, and no amount of sleep seems to make him feel rested. His wife has confronted him about his frequent temper tantrums, and his only solace seems to be in his after dinner drink or two or three . . .

Stress is a survival mechanism that helps us cope with new and different situations. It increases our attentiveness, effectiveness, and generally makes us more responsive to the environment. For example, imagine yourself driving down a one-way road when suddenly a car heads toward you at an incredible speed. You step on the brake and swerve your car just in time to avoid the oncoming car. Your reaction to stress helped increase your alertness and enabled you to react quickly to avoid a possible disaster. Stress can actually be good for the human body as long as it occurs in isolated episodes, is short lived, and is followed by recuperation time (Zuker, 1989). Stress becomes dangerous, however, when it extends over a long period of time and thus causes people to "burn out" (Walton, 1990). One characteristic of those who undergo unusual amounts of stress is that they often do not recognize the symptoms themselves. Because stress is a part of most people's lives, it is extremely difficult to tell when the amount of stress one is experiencing is healthy and when it is excessive. Some people may deny that they are "stressing out" because they are worried they will be labeled as psychologically weak or even neurotic. Unlike other types of diseases, stress is often overlooked or seen as something that "normal" individuals should be able to handle without outside help. What people overlook is that radical changes in the environment, such as moving abroad and adjusting to another culture, can be an extremely powerful stressor.

Holmes and Rahe's (1967) Social Readjustment Scale attaches numerical values to various changes people undergo during their lives. The most stressful change, according to this inventory, is the death of a spouse, which is given 100 points. Other changes, such as divorce (73 points), change in living conditions (25 points), change in residence (23 points), business readjustment (39 points), and change in recreation (19 points) that the same individual undergoes within a given year are added up. The assumption is that the levels of stress people experience are affected by the number and types of changes experienced simultaneously, and a score of 300 is considered high. People with scores in that range are considered to be vulnerable to stress-related problems. Shibusawa and Norton (1989) posit that, on average, people who move to Japan score at least 350 points. In fact, it can be assumed that virtually all sojourners will have at least 300 points according to this scale since moving entails various changes in one's life, such as a different workplace; a different residence; changes in one's social activities, recreation, and living conditions, as well as other environmental surroundings. This is based on the assumption that the individuals have not had other major changes in their lives, such as marriage (50 points), pregnancy (40 points), divorce (73 points), or other major life transitions. Individuals who have had major life transitions in addition to their move overseas, needless to say, are extremely susceptible to stress-related problems. Because this scale was based on domestic changes, it can be assumed that people on overseas assignments should be given a considerable number of additional points. The reason for this is that life in a foreign country is usually a succession of ambiguous situations with unfamiliar cues for the sojourner. Unpredictability, lack of certainty, and a general lack of control serve as stressors in their lives (Barna, 1983; Budner, 1962).

In summary, it can be said that sojourners and others who interact extensively with culturally different people undergo a significant amount of stress. Walton (1990) suggests that stress is an integral part of a sojourner's experience and that stress management should be incorporated into cross-cultural training programs. She suggests a three-step approach to stress-management training, namely: (a) presenting relevant content, (b) increasing coping options, and (c) practicing those options.

PRESENTING RELEVANT CONTENT

Trainees should become more aware of stress symptoms so that they can better understand the nature and unique aspects of stress that result from cross-cultural encounters. What follows are possible topics for lecture and discussion that should increase trainers' knowledge concerning stress.

Three common reactions that emerge from stressful situations are *fright, flight,* and *fight.* Imagine that you are scheduled to negotiate a major business contract with a Korean firm at 2:00 P.M. You have, however, a history of failed negotiation attempts with other Korean firms. It is now 1:30 P.M. You may note various symptoms of anxiety and *fright.* These symptoms may consist of pacing back and forth down the hall, sweaty palms, a dry mouth, or butterflies in your stomach. Some of you may actually feel a strong desire to disappear into midair and avoid the situation entirely *(flight).* On the other hand, some of you may feel a strong desire to get out there and *fight* your way through the contract (Zuker, 1989)!

To cope with these reactions toward stress, people can usually choose among three options. They can either change the situation that is causing the stress, change their attitude toward the situation, or accommodate to the stress (Shibusawa & Norton, 1989). In many cross-cultural encounters, people are placed in situations where they cannot do much to change the cause of their anxiety. As a result, they must change their attitude or accommodate to the stress. For example, an American who is "stressing out" in Mexico because everyone is always late for appointments cannot do much to change the situation. To persuade a whole country of people to be punctual would be a futile mission. Individuals who find themselves in this situation, therefore, either take on an "if you can't beat 'em, join 'em" attitude or learn to cope with the stress by arming themselves with books to read or work to do while waiting for people to arrive. *Defense mechanisms* are ways in which individuals psychologically accommodate to stress. Although some defense mechanisms are adaptive, others are not. *Adaptive defense mechanisms* are tools that help individuals cope with stress without distorting their perspectives. The single most important step in stress management is for individuals to recognize that they are, in fact, undergoing stress and to understand what is causing it. These people can then adopt healthy defense mechanisms such as humor, exercise, or volunteer work as a means of alleviating their stress. *Nonadaptive defense mechanisms* are those that distract the individuals from the problem at hand and instead create additional problems. Typical nonadaptive defense mechanisms are displacement, projection, rationalization, denial, repression, regression, passive-aggressive behavior, and acting out (all explained below). Although some are clearly more counterproductive than others, they all rob the individuals of the opportunity to face the stressful situation directly. Individuals who unconsciously employ some of these defense mechanisms are often not aware of the underlying reasons for their stress. In some cases, they are not even aware that they may be experiencing stress at all (Shibusawa & Norton, 1989)!

It should, therefore, be helpful for sojourners to be aware of the symptoms that characterize various defense mechanisms, in addition to other stress-related phenomena. Some of the symptoms that result from a short period of stress are restlessness, excessive smoking, low-grade infections, anxiety, tension, irritability, stuttering, an inability to concentrate, and fatigue (Zuker, 1989). If people experience these symptoms, they need to rest. Without rest, the symptoms develop further into others, such as uncontrolled anger, nervous tensions, sleeplessness, physical illness, withdrawal or denial, marital problems, depression, excessive eating, drinking, or smoking (Walton, 1990), migraines, stomachaches, dizziness, sweating, random behavior, lethargy, hypertension, indigestion, accident-proneness, chest pain, insomnia, depression, backache, eating irregularities, frigidity, impotence, fatigue, absenteeism, and reduced quantity and quality of work. These are signs that people are *not* coping well (Zuker, 1989). If these issues are not properly addressed, they may lead to tragic results such as heart attacks, ulcers, strokes, alcoholism, drug addiction, psychosis, suicide, or cancer. An example of people *displacing* their stress would be businesspeople frustrated with their work and taking it out on their spouses or children. An example of *projection* would be people who are suffering from large doses of stress but, instead of admitting it, are complaining excessively about *other people* being "edgy." When sojourners start to think that *all* host-country nationals are rude and inconsiderate or that *everyone* at work is short tempered lately, it is a possible sign that some form of projection may be taking place. *Rationalization* is perhaps one of the most commonly employed defense mechanisms, as well as one of the hardest to detect. People using it can logically convince themselves that some of their malfunctional behaviors are appropriate or inevitable. An example would be American sojourners in Japan who have found solace in drinking. They may notice that they are drinking excessively but may rationalize to themselves as well as to others that it is a necessary practice for people doing business in Japan. *Denial* and *repression* are also defense mechanisms that are hard to detect. Although technically denial refers to the immediate process of not admitting the existence of stress, if continued for an extended period of time it becomes *repression.* People who employ these strategies may psychosomatisize their stress, or, in extreme cases, may eventually suffer from a nervous breakdown. Sojourners should be aware of how their health has changed since their move and be careful to note any physical problems such as frequent headaches, insomnia, fatigue, stomach pains, and susceptibility to colds and flus. *Regression* is more commonly employed by children. Children undergoing stress sometimes revert to behaviors they should have outgrown. For example, children who are past the bed-wetting stage or the thumb-sucking stage may start wetting their beds or sucking their thumbs once again. Previously independent teenagers may revert to extreme dependence as a result of the move. An example of a *passive-aggressive* behavior would be children refusing to perform their chores or their homework. In other words, because they feel that overt expressions of their emotions such as anger or fear are inappropriate, they unconsciously divert their nervous energy through a different vehicle such as quiet rebelliousness. The final defense mechanism described by Shibusawa and Norton (1989) is *acting out*. If children have not been known to act out before the sojourn and have started to do so in the new environment, it is likely that it is being used to conceal a problem.

A common theme throughout the cross-cultural literature is that having realistic expectations and being able to anticipate stressful situations can help sojourners immensely as they undergo culture shock. The term *culture shock* was first used by Oberg (1960) to describe the anxiety that results from the general disorientation of not knowing appropriate behaviors and when to engage in them. When sojourners leave their home countries, they also leave behind friends, relatives, familiar activities, and clubs and organizations, as well as a whole society of people with similar values as themselves. Often, sojourners are not fully aware of the psychological consequences of such a large move. As a result, many suffer from mental strain, a sense of loss, confusion, surprise, anxiety, feelings of incompetence, and, in some cases, disgust and indignation toward host-country nationals (Furnham & Bochner, 1986; Oberg, 1960). At the beginning of their stay, the novelty of their new surroundings often clouds their perspectives and puts sojourners in a state of bliss. After a period of time, this initial state of excitement wears off and sojourners often feel rudely awakened by the reality of living in a society that is very different from their own. Many experience various symptoms of culture shock. Some that Oberg (1960) presents are

excessive washing of the hands; excessive concern over drinking water, food, dishes and bedding; fear of physical contact with attendants or servants; the absent-minded, far-away stare (sometimes called the "tropical stare"); a feeling of helplessness and a desire for dependence on long-term residents of one's own nationality; fits of anger over delays and other minor frustrations; delay and outright refusal to learn the language of the host country; excessive fear of being cheated, robbed, or injured; great concern over minor pains and irruptions of the skin; and finally, that terrible longing to be back home, to be able to have a good cup of coffee and a piece of apple pie, to walk into that corner drugstore, to visit one's relatives, and, in general, to talk to people who really make sense. (p. 176)

To further illustrate the stages that sojourners often go through, Gullahorn and Gullahorn (1963) presented the "U-curve hypothesis of cultural adjustment" as well as the "W-curve of cultural adjustment" (see Figure 3.1) that takes into consideration the reentry process. The U-curve hypothesis states that many sojourners go through a "honeymoon" period (Stage A) prior to their sojourn as well as at the beginning of their stay overseas. For some people this stage may last a few days while for others it may extend over a period of several months. During this time, people are in an elated state where everything appears wonderful. Following this stage is a state of disillusionment (Stage B) where sojourners start to recognize that things are very different from home. From here on, they start becoming more and more critical of the host country and carry strong feelings of resentment toward host-country nationals. According to the curve, these feelings intensify until the sojourners finally hit rock bottom (Stage C). At this point, they start to view their situation more realistically and notice positive aspects of the new culture (Stage D). With this realization comes a decrease in the level of stress experienced and a general feeling of contentment with their lives abroad. Unfortunately for many, this is when they are scheduled to return to their own countries. Upon arriving home, they once again go through the initial honeymoon stage (Stage F) where everything is idealized, followed by disillusionment (Stage G), and continuing through Steps H, I, and J in their own country. Numerous studies have found that the reentry process is often harder than the entry process because many sojourners idealize their home

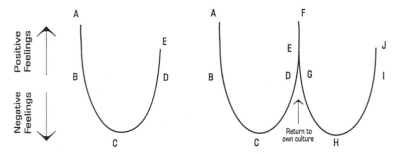

Figure 3.1. U and W-Shaped Curves of Adjustment

culture intensively while abroad, and because the gap between their expectations and reality tends to be much greater. Another interesting finding is that culture shock is actually a positive indicator that the sojourner is involved with the host culture. In other words, the extremely ethnocentric person would be less likely to notice cultural differences and therefore would not undergo culture shock. People should therefore work on managing the stress that it is caused by culture shock rather than trying to eliminate it (N. Adler, 1986).

Group discussions should help identify the various stressors that may play a significant role in the individuals' lives. In order to facilitate the discussion, trainers may wish to use Holmes and Rahe's Social Readjustment Scale or the list of stressful factors in the workplace presented by Zuker (1989, p. 165). Because neither of these is specific to cross-cultural situations, trainers may wish to use the 18 themes presented in the previous chapter as a supplement. By going down the list of themes, trainees may be able to identify numerous stressors in their lives.

INCREASING COPING OPTIONS

Once trainees are aware of the various symptoms of stress and are able to identify the types of stressors in their lives, the next step is to understand the types of coping options that are available to them. If trainees can comfortably change the situation that is causing the stress, that should be their first priority. For example, if language ability is the problem, the easiest and most effective way to reduce stress may be to take language lessons. If the situation cannot be changed, however, trainees can utilize one or both of the following methods. One is to cope *cognitively*. Because stress is not necessarily caused by events themselves but is the result of the one's perceptions of them, trying to reframe one's reactions toward difficult situations can effectively reduce stress. For example, arguments can be perceived either as emotionally draining or as intellectually stimulating. The second method is actively to form *social support* systems. Because moving overseas usually entails moving away from one's support systems such as friends, families, and community members, sojourners often have no one to turn to for help or assurance. Building a support system can therefore help individuals deal more effectively with everyday stresses that tend to be overwhelming in a foreign country.

Hardiness is a term that is often found in the stress literature. It is characterized by a strong positive attitude toward life in general, viewing stressful situations as challenges rather than obstacles, and maintaining a sense of control over various life events. Hardiness can help reduce stress, especially when combined with exercise (and Kobasa, Maddi, & Kahn, 1983; Kobasa, Maddi, & Puccetti, 1982). By consciously relabeling one's cognitions, changing one's appraisals of events, and improving one's sense of control, individuals should be able to acquire hardiness. For example, imagine an American who has found herself feeling frustrated with long and unproductive meetings at the Japanese company where she is working. One of the reasons she is feeling frustrated is probably linked to the fact that she has little or no control over the matter. Another possible reason for her frustration is that her definition and expectation of a meeting is most likely very different from that of her Japanese colleagues. For the American, a meeting should be short, simple, and straight to the point; discussions should be spontaneous and decisions should be made. For the Japanese (and the focus of her relabeling), however, meetings are more ritualistic. Decisions are always made in advance and meetings serve the purpose of solidifying the group by keeping everyone informed regarding the goings-on of the organization. By understanding this difference and approaching Japanese meetings with a different perspective, the American sojourner may be able to alleviate her stress to a certain degree. She may try reminding herself throughout meetings that the main purpose is to understand what other people are doing and that the meeting is successful as long as that objective is fulfilled. For many people, having realistic expectations can in itself foster a greater sense of personal control.

PRACTICING THOSE OPTIONS

Role-playing and simulations may be used to facilitate feelings of personal control. For example, instead of going to an actual meeting, the trainee may go to a simulated meeting made up of the rest of the training group. The advantage of using a simulation instead of using a real situation is that it is not as threatening in many regards. One characteristic of role-playing is that most trainees enjoy exaggerating their roles, leading to much laughter throughout the simulation. Trainees can practice over and over if needed. In addition, if they feel too frustrated, they can stop the simulation at any time. It is also recommended that trainees rank order situations that are stressful for them and start out with the least stressful ones and progressively move on to the more challenging.

◆ Practice During Training Programs: Examples

Social support is defined by House (1985) as an interaction between people that includes emotional concern, instrumental aid, information such as advice and suggestions, and appraisal. Fontaine (1986) suggests that social support systems can include family members, friends, neighbors, counselors, and work associates, as well as members of religious, recreational, and self-help groups. Once people leave home, they also leave their social support systems. Often sojourners are not aware of how integral to their well-being their support systems have been for them. Fontaine (1986) suggests that the disruption of people's support systems may be one of the primary sources of stress overseas. He recommends that people learn to identify their social support needs, recognize loss of previous support systems, and develop strategies for the creation of other support systems. In preparation, trainees should be encouraged during predeparture training to brainstorm areas where they can develop support systems immediately upon their arrival. Trainees are strongly discouraged from waiting until they are settled. One reason is that individuals are likely to need a support system the most immediately upon their arrival in a new country. Another reason is that sojourners will constantly be preoccupied by one thing or another and unless forced to do so, are unlikely to spend a considerable amount of time or effort on building a social support system for themselves.

As mentioned earlier, simulations and role-playing can be effective methods for practicing new cognitive strategies. Out of the various types of experiential learning methods, simulations usually rank highest in terms of stress level because of the intensity of interaction and the spontaneity involved. Open-ended role-playing is next in terms of intensity, followed by scripted role-playing, critical incidents, and finally small-group brainstorming exercises on personal coping strategies. Trainers need to be acutely aware of the degree of disclosure or risk with which specific training groups are comfortable. Trainers can either bore or put on the defensive many trainees depending on the compatibility of the exercises chosen.

Diet and *exercise* are often cited as effective stress fighters since stress is handled best if one is in good health. In addition, exercise is a good vehicle through which one's nervous energy can be expended in a healthy and socially acceptable manner. *Relaxation* is another effective strategy. Some people may prefer long warm baths with soothing music, while others may prefer transcendental meditation, and yet others may prefer using a programmed relaxation tape. Some people may feel the need to see a stress counselor or attend a stress-reduction retreat, and many self-help books are available on the market. Smith (1985) presents various exercises including scripts that people can read out to others. Because it is impossible to read and relax at the same time, it is recommended that people tape-record the exercises for later use. Instead of purchasing expensive tapes, many individuals find it more comforting to listen to their own voices once they are able to overcome the initial embarrassment. One of the exercises presented by Smith is called the thematic imagery exercise. The exercise takes approximately 20 minutes and helps individuals reach a deep state of relaxation through vivid suggestions of relaxing scenes such as a quiet beach, a grassy plain, or a cool mountain top. The exercise is suitable for the beginner because it continuously provides the listener with guidance on which of the senses to focus. The excerpt below represents a portion of the exercise.

> And now, quietly let your mind dwell on this scene for the next few seconds (pause 15 seconds) . . . Let the scene become as vivid and real as possible. (pause 10 seconds) . . . How does it look? (pause 10 seconds) . . . Can you see the sky? (pause) . . . Can you feel the wind brushing against your skin? (pause) . . . Can you smell the gentle, cool air? . . . (Smith, 1985, pp. 167-170)

◆ Conclusion

Cross-cultural encounters cause people to experience emotional arousal. When people are not able to deal effectively with high levels of emotional arousal, they can experience stress that may damage their health. Although people's ability to deal with their feelings and emotions strongly influences the level of effectiveness and success they achieve overseas, it is rarely given enough attention in cross-cultural training sessions. Often, employing organizations as well as the sojourners themselves assume that stress is a personal issue with which healthy individuals should be able to cope effectively. As mentioned earlier, sojourners undergo numerous changes simultaneously, making them highly susceptible to stress-related problems. Mike, for example, who was introduced earlier in the chapter, was handling his assignment in Honduras successfully and was effectively interacting with co-workers. His problem, however, was that he was unable to recognize the considerable amount of stress he was experiencing in the process of adjusting to his new position as a branch president as well as to the Honduran culture in general. Prolonged episodes of stress may lead to unfortunate results. In Mike's case, one result may be alcohol abuse. We strongly recommend that more attention be given to emotional challenges and stress management in future training programs. People's perception of the degree of control they have over important events is closely linked to the amount of their perceived stress. The next chapter will concentrate on skills and recommend behaviors that will help trainees function more effectively and thus gain stronger feelings of self-efficacy concerning their intercultural encounters.

Note

1. Trifonovitch conducted preservice training programs for Peace Corps volunteers assigned to posts in Micronesia. Out of the 600 participants, most of them were American educators in their thirties along with their families. Most of them had several years of teaching experience and had not been out of the continental United States before this assignment. The programs lasted 2 to 3 weeks, and the training staff consisted mostly of native Micronesians from the various island groups or districts in addition to a small number of Americans with cross-cultural experience. Training was conducted in rural Oahu, Molokai, or Moen (Truk district), and the environments were created to resemble the living environments in Micronesia as much as possible.

4

Acquiring Intercultural Communication Skills

◆ The Asian Expert

Jim is the chair of the counseling psychology department at a small university on the east coast. In addition to 5 years of previous work experience in Japan, Jim has been actively involved with international students at the university. When his schedule permits, he often gives intercultural communication training workshops for university faculty and staff. His American colleagues often turn to him for advice and regard him as the university's Asian expert. Jim knows the cross-cultural literature well and often talks of the need to tolerate ambiguity and to be nonjudgmental. He often uses critical incidents to demonstrate how even the best of intentions can lead to misunderstandings if individuals are not aware of the culture of the people with whom they are interacting. Jim often refers to cultural relativity as a key concept in adjusting to a new country and encourages trainees to be as open-minded as possible.

One day, Jim called Keiko, a Japanese graduate student, to come in for an evaluation meeting. Keiko entered the counseling psychology department two semesters ago as a full-time student and was not doing well. The professors felt that she lacked initiative because she refused to take any of the classes that involved active participation and actual counseling experience. Although they understood that her English was minimal, they felt that it would not improve unless she made an effort to do so. At the meeting, they were to discuss whether she should continue with the program or not. Also attending the meeting was a bilingual Japanese student, whom Jim asked to serve as the interpreter.

> **Jim:** Thank you for taking time out of your busy schedules today. As I told you beforehand, today we are here to decide whether it would be wiser for Keiko to stay or whether it would be better for her to choose a different career path. (To the interpreter) I'm not sure if she understands what is going on so could you please explain that to her?
>
> **Int:** Sure (explains in Japanese) . . . she says she was perfectly aware of all of this . . .
>
> **Jim:** Oh, really! I guess she understands more English than I gave her credit for! Well . . . could you ask her what she thinks?
>
> **Int:** Sure . . . (explains in Japanese) . . ."
>
> **Keiko:** (breathes in, looks down, and appears to be thinking)
>
> **Jim:** Yes???
>
> **Int:** She's still thinking . . .
>
> **Jim:** But what is there to think about??? Didn't she think about all this before she came in?
>
> **Keiko:** (slowly and haltingly) I would like to stay and give it a try . . .
>
> **Jim:** (jumps right in) All right, Keiko, you can . . . but you're going to either have to take one of the counseling practice classes or take an intensive English course, all right?
>
> **Keiko:** (again looks down, has a small frown on her face, and appears to be thinking)
>
> **Jim:** You know that all of your professors have been trying their hardest to accommodate to you, don't you? We've let you audit classes for the past two semesters, but unless you start taking them for credit you will be wasting everyone's time, including your own . . .
>
> **Keiko:** (is still looking down, takes a deep breath and opens her mouth . . .)

Jim: Will you please say something? This silence is driving me
nuts! It's been half an hour already and we haven't accomplished
anything! (To the interpreter) Are you sure she understands what
I've been saying to her???

In this case study, Jim misinterprets Keiko's silence for ignorance. Keiko, on the other hand, is unaware that her silence is
being perceived negatively. Rather, she is using it to show respect.
Her pauses should have indicated to Jim that his questions were
important enough to require much thought. To answer a question immediately without hesitation in Japan would be insulting
because it would mean that the question is so simple it did not
require any thought. If presented as a case study, Jim would more
than likely understand what went wrong during his interview
with Keiko. Finding himself in the midst of this situation,
however, Jim is unable to display cultural sensitivity.

Understanding the theories and concepts in intercultural communication does not automatically lead to culturally sensitive
behaviors. In fact, it is not uncommon to find individuals who
are extremely knowledgeable about theories regarding cross-
cultural effectiveness, who possess the best of intentions, yet
who are unable to demonstrate their knowledge in their actions
(Koester & Olebe, 1988; Ruben & Kealey, 1979). As mentioned
in an earlier analogy in Chapter 2, people who are *aware* of the
need to take swimming lessons, understand the basic ideas behind swimming *(knowledge),* and have overcome *emotional*
barriers are still unable to swim! The prior steps are necessary,
but alone are insufficient to make competent swimmers. In the
same way, people who are aware, emotionally prepared, and
knowledgeable about cross-cultural issues are not necessarily
competent communicators until they also have practiced the
appropriate skills.

Skills training in the intercultural communication field has
been a controversial issue. Instilling such skills as the proper way
to bow or pour tea or shake hands can be counterproductive if
not accompanied by appropriate information regarding the culture. For example, American businesspeople who bow and greet

their Chinese counterparts without understanding the Chinese culture can find themselves in trouble. If the Americans were to make a cultural faux pas, the Chinese might interpret it as being intentional rather than giving them the benefit of the doubt. In addition, if the Americans were not aware of how to show deference according to status through their greetings, their well-intentioned attempts might instead create ill-feelings.

Many trainers hesitate to prescribe specific behaviors because they believe that advocating one over another is in itself attaching a value judgment, contradicting the general notion of cultural relativity. Some trainers simply avoid the issue because of defensive trainees who dislike being told what to do. The problem with skirting the issue by not addressing actual skills is that it can lead to two possible consequences. One is that trainees may become frustrated because they have become painfully aware of their culturally inappropriate behaviors without knowing *how* to change them. Another possible outcome is that people may perceive themselves as being culturally sensitive because they are so well versed in the literature when, in fact, their behaviors are not reflective of their knowledge. Jim, who was introduced at the beginning of this chapter, is a good example of the latter. With his knowledge of the Japanese culture, he should have known that Keiko's silence carried a deliberate message and was not a reflection of her ignorance. Long periods of silence can evoke strong emotional reactions for many Americans. Cognitive understanding, therefore, is not enough. People must actively develop the skill of using, as well as interpreting, silence.

As mentioned in Chapter 2, time and budget constraints are extremely important issues with which many trainers must contend. *Awareness* and *emotions* need to be added to the standard training curriculum of *knowledge* and *skills,* and many programs fall short of covering all four stages. We suggest that trainees go through all four stages in some form or another. For this reason, needs assessments are crucial in determining the stages in which trainees find themselves. In some cases, trainees may be culturally aware and knowledgeable and simply need skills training. In other cases, trainees may require a more full-scale (i.e., all four stages) training program. Because time is such a constraint, teaching trainees how to acquire knowledge and skills *on their own* is considered by many trainers and researchers as a crucial component of a good training program. This enables trainees to further develop their cross-cultural competence through their everyday lives and continue to grow and develop their skills. This chapter will cover two types of skills training: culture general and culture specific.

◆ Culture-General Skills

Certain skills, such as the ability to tolerate ambiguity, manage stress, establish realistic expectations, and demonstrate flexibility and empathy are helpful tools in all types of cross-cultural adjustment. In this section, we will review three examples of culture-general skills development, namely, the use of: (1) the Cross-Cultural Adaptability Inventory, (2) Hofstede's dimensions applied to the adjustment of international students, and (3) the intercultural sensitivity inventory.

CROSS-CULTURAL ADAPTABILITY INVENTORY

Using the Cross-Cultural Adaptability Inventory (CCAI; Kelley & Meyers, 1992a), trainees first assess their strengths and weaknesses through a self-report inventory and are then provided with an action-planning guide that suggests exercises and strategies to help expand their skills. The inventory is divided into four dimensions, namely: (a) emotional resilience, (b) flexibility and openness, (c) perceptual acuity, and (4) personal autonomy.

Emotional resilience refers to individuals' ability to maintain a positive emotional state *regardless* of the many obstacles they may encounter overseas. Ability to handle large amounts of stress, ambiguity, and strong emotions characterize this trait. In addition, self-confidence and a positive self-image are also linked to emotional resilience. In general, the *ability* to maintain a positive outlook on life and to "bounce back," even after a series of major let-downs, is measured. The following is one of the activities recommended for people who need to work on developing this trait further.

> When you experience difficult feelings, especially when you are with others different from yourself or in an unfamiliar setting, pay attention to your underlying thoughts. What are you telling yourself in order to create those feelings? Find more useful and positive things to say to yourself, and practice saying them. Practice doing something that makes you feel better. Keep a journal of positive statements about yourself, and use it as a resource during difficult times. Place the statements in places where you will see them often. (Kelley & Meyers, 1992b, p. 3)

Flexibility and openness are characterized by accepting other ways of doing things, a lack of rigidity, and an ethnorelative perspective. People who score high on this trait are able to adapt to many different cultures because they do not believe in, or feel compelled to, stick to the "one and only truth." What follows is one of the exercises prescribed for people who seek further development in this trait.

> Interact with people who are different from yourself, who do not share your interests, or who think differently than you do. Find out more about them. Identify things which you like about them. If you find yourself becoming judgmental about how they are different from you, find a way to appreciate the differences, and identify ways in which you are like them. (Kelley & Meyers, 1992b, p. 4)

Perceptual acuity refers to the degree of sensitivity individuals have in terms of verbal and nonverbal messages, as well as to interpersonal relations in general. Although a particular behavior may reflect different messages across cultures, the more sensitive individuals are to those messages, the more likely they are to understand the different meanings attached to them in other cultures. Individuals who are perceptually acute are aware of how their actions influence others and are sensitive to other people's emotions. When people communicate across cultures, they are at a disadvantage. Often they do not hold the same values, nor have they undergone similar socialization experiences. Therefore, when they communicate, an unusual amount of sensitivity is necessary. The following exercise is aimed at developing this skill.

Observe others' body language in reaction to what you say and to your own body language. This includes gestures, tone of voice, pace of speaking, facial expression, posturing, and so on. Body language may be interpreted totally differently from what you intend to communicate. Ask questions about this if necessary, to be sure you are "speaking the same language." It may also be helpful to videotape and/or audio tape yourself, and observe your own body language or listen to your own ways of speaking. (Kelley & Meyers, 1992b, p. 5)

Personal autonomy is the extent to which individuals feel comfortable with their own self-identities. When people cross cultural boundaries, many of their values and beliefs are challenged. People can no longer rely on their culture to reaffirm their self-worth, but must instead have an independent sense of identity that they can maintain regardless of the culture in which they find themselves. Although it is not possible for individuals to have a sense of identity that is completely independent of their culture's value systems, it is crucial for them to understand that having their values challenged is not synonymous with having their identities challenged. For this reason, personal autonomy, which refers to the individual's sense of identity, is extremely important. One of the exercises suggested in Kelley and Meyers' action plan is as follows.

Clarify your personal values. Make a rank-ordered list of what you stand for or what is genuinely important to you. Examples of values include privacy, love, money, loyalty, and honesty. Identify those things that mean most in life to you and what makes them so important to you. (Kelley & Meyers, 1992b, p. 6)

The CCAI was not devised for the purpose of selecting people who will perform well in other cultures. Instead, it is an inventory that is designed to promote further growth and development in intercultural understanding for interested individuals. One of the advantages of the CCAI is that it addresses many culture-general skills that were previously considered personality traits. By treating these as skills that can be acquired instead of as personality characteristics, which are perceived to be less flexible, the CCAI provides a constructive means by which individuals can develop culture-general skills. Another feature of this inventory is its transparency. Items are fairly obvious and are clearly related to the four dimensions. One of the advantages is that it can be scored by anyone. Individuals can go back and change their responses at any time. If desired, people can take the inventory in the privacy of their homes. One of the disadvantages of transparency is that because the socially desirable answers are obvious, people may be more prone to distort their answer choices. Another problem with a self-assessment is that people's perceptions of themselves may differ from the way others perceive them. One of the ways in which the CCAI tries to alleviate this problem is by having three people who know the participants well fill out "feedback forms." The feedback forms cover the same questions as the inventory itself. Participants can therefore use them as reality checks or as a validations of their self-perceptions.

HOFSTEDE'S DIMENSIONS APPLIED TO
THE ADJUSTMENT OF INTERNATIONAL STUDENTS

As a result of an extensive survey of more than 116,000 people from more than 40 different countries, Hofstede (1980) arrived at his four-dimensional model of cultural differences. The dimensions were: (a) individualism and collectivism, (b) power distance, (c) uncertainty avoidance, and (d) masculinity and femininity. In his subsequent writing, Hofstede (1986) applied his four concepts to student-teacher interactions, specifying behavioral ramifications for each of the dimensions. His model was later expanded to add a fifth dimension called "Confucian dynamism" (Hofstede & Bond, 1988). Here, we would like to examine how some of the behaviors noted by Hofstede can be included in a skills training program for international students as well as for their professors. In addition, we would like to include Confucian dynamism in our discussion as well. The goal of this discussion is to identify the *specific behaviors and skills* that teachers and students can learn in order to facilitate effective cross-cultural interactions.

People who are socialized in a culture where *individualism* is the norm tend to make a sharp distinction between the self and society. Independence and self-reliance are looked upon with favor while dependence is often viewed as a sign of immaturity. Because individuals are perceived to be "out there fending for themselves," emphasis is placed on such values as competition, utilitarianism, and exchanges (helping the community only if one gets something in return) (Bellah et al., 1985, p. 26). Attorneys, psychiatrists, and homes for the elderly are reflections of exchange relationships. In most collectivist cultures, these are roles (e.g., good listener, elderly parents' caretaker) that friends and family members fill. In cultures where the idealized vision of the "rugged individual" exists, however, people see time as money. In these cultures, people must fend for themselves and be responsible for their own lives. Consequently, it is an unwarranted imposition on others to expect them to listen to our problems or act as a mediator when they could in fact be earning money for themselves. In the same way, many elderly people feel it is an imposition to expect their children to take care of them in their old age. Instead, these individuals choose to exchange money for these services. By depersonalizing these relationships individuals no longer feel dependent on other people, but instead must develop a strong sense of independence.

People who are socialized in a culture where *collectivism* is valued, however, do not draw as clear a distinction between self and society. They view interdependence as important and foster it through children's socialization processes. For example, it is not unusual to find unmarried Korean adults living with their parents. It is also customary for the elderly to expect their children to live with and take care of them. In many collectivist cultures psychiatrists and counselors do not have a prominent niche in society because friends and family provide the support that individuals need. Relatives and friends also provide other services such as finding a marriage partner or a job.

Three of Hofstede's differences between individualist and collectivist societies warrant extended discussion.

Positive association in society with whatever is rooted in tradition (collectivist) versus positive association in society with whatever is "new" (individualist) (Hofstede, 1986, p. 312).

American foreign exchange students are sometimes shocked to find that in many countries books that are considered outdated by most American scholars are still studied. On the other hand, many international exchange students are often shocked to find that American students are ignorant of the classic research conducted in their fields of interest and are only familiar with that which is most current. Understanding these concepts can lead to various behavioral strategies. One possibility is for American professors to increase their credibility with their collectivist students by emphasizing the fact that they, too, are aware of the classics but have *chosen* to pursue further the more current research. Collectivist students might want to take a similar approach. Instead of ignoring the most current research entirely they should acknowledge its existence before pursuing what they believe is important.

Education is a way of gaining prestige in one's social environment and of joining a higher status group (collectivist) versus education is a way of improving one's economic worth and self-respect based on ability and competence (individualist) (Hofstede, 1986, p. 312).

Many American college professors who find themselves in Japan are surprised by the "laziness" of their students. In general, American college professors view academia as a place for students to acquire more knowledge, become more competent, and therefore more employable. For many Japanese, however, the most intense years of their education ends upon graduation from high school. Their college education counts most in terms of the name value of their university and the contacts they make through the school (i.e., alumni). Many collectivist students, immediately prior to graduation from an American university, find to their shock and dismay that alumni from their institutions provide little or no support with their job placement. Students from collectivist cultures should be encouraged to make contacts outside of the university setting instead of expecting a ready-made network to be available to them upon entering a university. American professors, on the other hand, must make a point of discussing the limited role of alumni in job placement in American settings at the *beginning* of their collectivist students' university education. By explaining that networking through professional organizations, community activities, and internships perform the role that university alumni in collectivist countries play, professors can help students make the most of their education in the United States. Developing *one's own networks* is extremely important to functioning well in the American social system (Brislin, 1991).

Neither the teacher nor the student should ever be made to lose face (collectivist) versus face-consciousness is weak (individualist) (Hofstede, 1986, p. 312).

Face-saving is another behavior that is fostered in collectivist societies, though not as valued in individualist societies. Many collectivist students will not challenge their professors because they do not want them to "lose face." American professors, on the other hand, expect and respect students who challenge their views to a certain extent, perceiving them as interested and involved. Collectivist students should therefore be encouraged to overcome the hesitation they might have with regard to challenging their professors. Professors should also learn to appreciate their students' attempt to "save their face" instead of evaluating them as uninterested or passive.

Power distance is the degree to which social hierarchy is considered acceptable or even desirable within various societies. Although social inequities exist in all cultures, some are more tolerant of them than others. Individuals in large power distance countries are more resigned to social inequity and accept it as part of reality. Those in small power distance cultures, in general, carry a more egalitarian ideal.

In large power distance cultures (e.g., Philippines, Malaysia, Panama), teachers are treated with utmost respect and deference due to their societal role. In contrast, teachers in low power distance cultures (e.g., Austria, Israel, New Zealand, the United States) are looked upon as fallible human beings who are perhaps more knowledgeable but do not demand any more respect than do their students. When students from high power distance countries come to the United States for their college or graduate education many are surprised at the disrespectfulness of other students. The casual and egalitarian manner of the professors (e.g., lecturing in a T-shirt) is often interpreted as a lack of professionalism and credibility. Many also find themselves at a loss at the lack of guidance they receive from their professors. A common phenomenon is for these students to do outstandingly well until it is time to write their final thesis or their dissertation. This is often called "The Great Wait" because professors often find themselves waiting for the students to take the initiative with their thesis or dissertation topic while the students often wait for their professors to assign a topic to them. This can, in some cases, delay a student's date of graduation by a few years (as discussed in Chapter 1).

Teachers and professors who have students from low power distance cultures in their classes may want to keep in mind some of the behaviors listed by Hofstede. One that deserves extended discussion is: "Teacher expects students to initiate communication (small power distance) versus students expect teachers to initiate communication (large power distance)" (Hofstede, 1986, p. 313). American professors and teachers can make an effort to call on students from collectivist cultures to answer questions during class instead of expecting them to take the initiative and respond to a general invitation. On the other hand, if professors feel that it is the student's responsibility to adapt to the American educational system, they can help them acquire certain skills such as taking the initiative and asking questions in class, criticizing the teacher when appropriate, and maintaining two-way conversations with professors. Teachers and professors must, however, remember that these behaviors are deeply rooted in these students' values and beliefs and changing them is not an easy process (Hofstede, 1986). Being supportive and providing substantial positive reinforcements are therefore essential.

To illustrate the difficulty students from high power distance countries encounter when expected to adjust to the American educational system, it might be helpful to visualize the opposite. Imagine several American students placed in a high power distance country where they are told to listen passively and not argue with the teachers. These students are likely to rebel against these instructions because they believe that it is simply not the "right" or "best" way to conduct class. Because many of our behavioral patterns are not arbitrary but are strongly linked to our beliefs of what is right and wrong, changing or adapting new behaviors can often be very difficult though essential. In the same way that a passive student is viewed as lacking initiative in a low power distance culture, an egalitarian teacher is likely to have little credibility in a high power distance culture.

Uncertainty avoidance refers to the amount of tolerance people have with regard to ambiguity. If people prefer ritualistic and predictable behaviors and many rules, they are considered to be strong in uncertainty avoidance. On the other hand, if they thrive on spontaneity and change, they are considered to be low in uncertainty avoidance. Strong uncertainty avoidance societies (e.g., Greece, Portugal, Japan) tend to have an abundance of rules and rituals that help preserve a comfortable amount of predictability in people's lives. For example, when invited to a wedding, Japanese individuals *know* that in their country money is the appropriate gift to bring. They also know approximately how much to bring depending on their status and their relationship to the bride and the groom. It is therefore very easy for individuals to act in a socially appropriate manner.

If one were invited to a wedding in the United States (low uncertainty avoidance), however, one must choose from a spectrum of possible gift items. Although there are certain guidelines to follow, they are not nearly as rigid as the Japanese rules. Gift-giving, like many other social interactions, requires more spontaneity and risk-taking in low uncertainty avoidance societies.

The following is an example of a difference that is rooted in the amount of uncertainty avoidance prevalent in different countries.

Students feel comfortable in unstructured learning situations: vague objectives, broad assignments, no timetables (weak uncertainty avoidance) versus students feel comfortable in structured learning situations: precise objectives, detailed assignments, strict timetables (strong uncertainty avoidance) (Hofstede, 1986, p. 314).

Many international students who come from strong uncertainty avoidance cultures find themselves at a loss when professors assign them to do a group project on a topic of their own choice with anyone in the class. Many of these students are used to a more structured environment where both their topic and their group members are assigned to them by their professors. A strategy professors might take is to provide a list of topics covered in the past as well as suggestions of other possible topic areas. If the professor introduces the students to possible collaborators, it will most likely be extremely well received. Another problem many students from high uncertainty avoidance cultures face at American universities is caused by the heavy emphasis placed on class discussions. Because class discussions appear too spontaneous, involving a great amount of risk and a possible loss of face, many of these students hesitate to participate even when their language skills are excellent.

The *masculinity and femininity* dimension refers to whether the society as a whole advocates what Hofstede defines as characteristically "male" or "female" values. High masculinity cultures make a clear distinction between the "male" and "female" roles. Males are expected to be assertive, ambitious, and willing to compete for material success. Females, on the other hand, are supposed to be nurturing, soft, and weak. Male and female roles are less clearly defined in cultures that rank high in femininity. It is therefore socially acceptable for men to care about feelings and other nonmaterialistic aspects of life.

Students from high masculinity cultures (i.e., Japan, Austria, Venezuela) are likely to be much more competitive in class than those from high femininity cultures (i.e., the Scandinavian countries). Consequently, teachers from high masculinity cultures are likely to reinforce competitive behavior by openly praising good students. Teachers from high femininity cultures, on the other hand, are more likely to reinforce the average but cooperative student (Hofstede, 1986). Because the United States ranks somewhere in the middle but more toward the masculinity side, international students who come from extreme ends of the continuum may need to acquaint themselves with the amount of competitiveness and cooperation that is expected in U.S. classrooms. Professors and teachers can help by being very explicit about their expectations. This can be helpful not only for international students, but also for students who come from different departments. For example, students in the counseling department are likely to rank higher in femininity than MBA students. When conducting a class where students from both departments attend, professors should be aware of the differences in cooperativeness and competitiveness in the two "cultures."

Confucian dynamism was later added as Hofstede's fifth dimension (Chinese Culture Connection, 1987; Hofstede & Bond, 1988). The concept was developed to help explain the tremendous economic growth experienced in recent years by the "five dragons" (i.e., Japan, South Korea, Hong Kong, Taiwan, and Singapore). Some of the outstanding characteristics of Confucian dynamism will be discussed in the following paragraphs. One of the key beliefs in countries that rank high in Confucian dynamism is the importance of unequal status relationships. Relationships such as those between parents and children, teachers and students, mentors and mentorees, and even those between older and younger students, are all clearly hierarchical.

In exchange for deference and respect from their "juniors," "seniors" are expected to take good care and provide helpful guidance to them. In general, their relationships are marked by mutual obligations.

Another characteristic of Confucian dynamism is that hard work and perseverance are looked upon very highly. Instead of glorifying the genius, the diligent, thrifty, and perseverant person is exalted. If people lack persistence, they experience a strong sense of shame for not trying hard enough. Because the *amount* of work they do affects not only themselves but their families and the rest of society, the sense of shame functions as a strong motivator. Another value that is supported by Confucianism is a concern for the future. This is closely linked to the idea of "unequal status relationships." As mentioned earlier, once individuals are "senior" members of a relationship they become responsible for the well-being of their "junior" members. These "junior" members are most likely "senior" members in a different relationship, making them obligated to take care of their "juniors" as well. Through this continuing linkage with the rest of society, individuals' consciousness of the future is fostered.

A possible way in which the amount of Confucian dynamism might affect classroom situations would be the importance attached to diligence and perseverance in contrast to simple assessments of the final product. Teachers and professors from high Confucian dynamism countries are likely to applaud the average child who shows an extraordinary amount of perseverance. Professors from lower Confucian dynamism cultures may, on the other hand, be shocked and surprised at the extreme dedication some of their students from Taiwan or Korea may show. They may even feel that the amount of effort put in is excessive and even damaging to individuals' health and well-being. Some of these professors may feel that the students are inefficient with their time and should learn time management, instead of applauding them for the amount of effort and persistence they have displayed.

INTERCULTURAL SENSITIVITY INVENTORY

Unlike the CCAI, which was not developed for selection purposes, the Intercultural Sensitivity Inventory (ICSI; Bhawuk & Brislin, 1992) can be used to distinguish those who have high intercultural sensitivity from those who do not. In addition, because the items address specific behaviors, individuals can use the results of the inventory as a guideline to develop their skills further.

The ICSI is a 46-item inventory. Approximately half the questions focus on individualism and collectivism issues (Hofstede, 1980), and the other half address flexibility and open-mindedness. The first 16 items aim at measuring behavioral adaptability across the individualism-collectivism continuum. Participants are instructed to imagine that they are living and working in the United States while answering the first 16 questions. They are then instructed to visualize themselves living and working in Japan while answering the same set of questions again. Although the United States and Japan are suggested as examples, participants are encouraged to select countries with which they are most familiar. For example, Australian participants with extensive experiences in Indonesia might choose first to answer the first 16 questions based on how they would behave in Australia and the next 16 based on how they would act in Indonesia. This section of the instrument measures individuals' perceptions of whether they are able to change their *behaviors* according to the cultural settings in which they find themselves. The remainder of the inventory focuses on flexibility and open-mindedness. Bhawuk and Brislin (1992) concluded that the results from the flexibility and open-mindedness section were not as clear (in terms of the clarity of the two concepts) as those from the individualism and collectivism portion of the inventory. They suggested further research with regard to the flexibility and open-mindedness concepts but also asserted that the quality of the instrument was improved by their inclusion.

One of the advantages of the ICSI is that it addresses specific behaviors related to individualism and collectivism. Too often such concepts are left in the abstract where their practical applications can be unclear to the uninitiated. Individualism and collectivism are by far the best investigated and least controversial of the five concepts presented by Hofstede (Schwartz, 1990; Triandis, Brislin, & Hui, 1988). The items presented in the ICSI are explicit and can therefore be used by individuals as guidelines for behavioral changes. Some of the items used in the inventory are:

Individualism Items
   a. When I disagree with a group, I would allow a conflict in the group to remain, rather than change my own stance on important issues.
   b. I prefer to be direct and forthright when dealing with people.
   c. To increase sales I would announce that the individual salesperson with the highest sales would be given the "Distinguished Salesperson" award.

Collectivism Items
   d. I enjoy developing long-term relationships among the people with whom I work.
   e. I am very modest when talking about my own accomplishments.
   f. If I want a person to perform a certain task I try to show how the task will benefit others in the person's group (Bhawuk & Brislin, 1992).

The participants' scores on the first 16 responses (behaviors they think they would display in an individualistic culture) are compared to their second 16 (behaviors they think they would display in a collectivist culture). Participants with higher scores are more likely to change their behaviors according to the cultural norms in which they find themselves, hence should be more effective than those with lower scores. For example, they would answer items a, b, and c with "yes" when imagining themselves in an individualist culture, but "no" when imagining themselves in a collectivist culture. The results can then be used by participants as a basis for their own skills development plan. For example, certain trainees may realize that despite their cognitive understanding of the importance of consensus in collectivist cultures, they are unable to restrain themselves from asserting what they believe is the "truth" even among collectivist colleagues. Trainees not only need to convince themselves on the intellectual level but must also practice restraining themselves in situations where they would otherwise be tempted to voice their opinions and break up a consensus. On the other hand, certain trainees who find themselves leaning toward the collectivist end of the continuum may note that they are equally modest in both cultures. They may also realize that their modesty may have cost them several promotions in an individualist society since no one at work was aware of their accomplishments. These trainees can then make an effort to assert themselves in a socially appropriate manner when in an individualist culture (suggestions for this made in Brislin, 1991).

Up to this point, culture-general skills have been discussed. To introduce the equally central topic of culture-specific skills, an important study will be discussed.

◆ Culture-Specific Skills

Collett (1971) conducted an experiment in which he trained British subjects to adopt Arab nonverbal mannerisms. The subjects were given very specific instructions.

1. When you are introduced to your Arab partner, rise to your feet, then shake hands while lowering your head slightly. Nod and smile, all the time looking him in the eyes. 2. Once you have both sat down, pull your chair toward the Arab's so that, with your arm extended, you could touch his chest. Do not take up the out-of-reach distance that we usually adopt when we meet strangers. 3. Arabs always sit "straight on," instead of orienting themselves away from the interactor as we so often do. Try to do likewise. 4. Although you may find it rather strange at first, it is important that you look the Arab constantly in the eyes while talking to him. Avoid

averting your gaze at all costs, as Arabs feel more comfortable when there is more mutual looking . . . (p. 210)

A trained subject and a control subject were then asked to enter a room and carry on a 5-minute conversation about love with an Arab. After the two Englishmen left the room, the Arab subject was asked to make a variety of sociometric choices between the two men, in addition to writing a few paragraphs about the encounter. A total of 10 trials with different subjects were conducted. The results of the experiment revealed that Arabs showed a much stronger liking toward the trained English subjects compared to those of the control group. This suggests that adopting behavioral patterns of the host culture can facilitate effective interpersonal relationships.

Trainers must, however, take certain precautions when prescribing culture-specific skills. If these skills are not used with sufficient foresight or cultural knowledge, the following outcomes may occur. One possibility is for trainees to be trapped in a stereotype, unable to see the uniqueness of the particular individuals with whom they interact. The other possibility is that trainees might use their newly acquired skills indiscriminately in appropriate as well as inappropriate social situations. We therefore recommend the following steps when including culture-specific skills in a cross-cultural training program.

1. Identify a skill (or a set of skills) that should facilitate better communication with people from a specific culture.
2. Understand why this skill is important. Examine the cultural value(s) attached to this skill.
3. Find out when, where, and how this skill is appropriately used. This can be done through interviews with resource people, observing everyday interactions between these people, or through watching television programs and movies. Television shows and movies provide trainees with an easily accessible source of invaluable cultural phenomena. Trainees must, however, be careful not to overgeneralize or believe everything they see on the screen.
4. Understand that there are individual differences within all societies. Even if a particular behavior is considered the "norm" in a certain society, there is always the possibility the individual you

are interacting with does not subscribe to it. Make sure you are conscious of the uniqueness of the individual with whom you are interacting. Don't stereotype!
5. Practice this skill in day-to-day interaction with people from the host culture.

Tables 4.1 and 4.2 list culture-specific behaviors that can be used in training programs. To facilitate usage, we have reframed the cultural traits cited in the literature into behavioral strategies Americans can practice to improve their communication skills with culturally different others. These behaviors are arranged by country and are by no means comprehensive, but should provide readers with the basic ideas behind our approach. Table 4.1 lists behaviors that Americans can adopt to facilitate communication with people from various countries. Table 4.2 lists behaviors that Anglo-Americans can adopt when interacting with members of certain ethnic groups in the United States.

◆ An Approach to Learning Culture-Specific Behaviors: The Skill-Streaming Approach

The Skill-Streaming or Structured Learning Approach was originally developed to help long-term, skill-deficient patients in mental institutions acquire various interpersonal and daily survival skills that would help deinstitutionalize them. It was then modified with a new focus on (noninstitutionalized) aggressive individuals. One of the premises of this approach is that many people who display antisocial skills *do not know how* to act in a prosocial manner. Many individuals who *are* socially adept learn these skills by observing their parents and other people in their environment. When they experiment with various behaviors, they find that they are rewarded for some but not for others. These people thus acquire what that society considers "prosocial skills." Many aggressive individuals learn antisocial skills in the same manner. For example,

TABLE 4.1
International Dimension of Intercultural Behaviors

	Behaviors Americans Can Adopt When Interacting With . . .
Germans	1. Become more knowledgeable in world history, philosophy, geography, and politics.
	2. Practice conducting intense discussion on the above topics. Voices may become emotional! Learn to be comfortable with such intense discussions (Items 1 & 2 from Friday, 1989).
	3. Practice calling the other party by his or her title. Don't insist on being called or calling the other party by first name prematurely (Friday, 1989; Hall, 1983)!
Japanese	1. When in doubt, apologize! Practice apologizing *directly* without making any excuses. Because apologizing is considered an admission of guilt for many Americans, they feel the need to defend themselves by making excuses. In Japan, however, apologies are used as social lubricants. People apologize for the inconveniences they have caused, not for the actual behaviors. Because the Japanese will not use an apology to incriminate someone, Americans should feel more comfortable with making direct apologies (Barnlund & Yoshioka, 1990; Naotsuka, Sakamoto et al., 1981; Sakamoto & Naotsuka, 1982).
	2. Practice being indirect (Harris & Moran, 1987; Naotsuka, Sakamoto et al., 1981; Sakamoto & Naotsuka, 1982).
	3. Learn how to tell when someone is saying "no" to you. Also learn how to say "no" without insulting the other party (Ueda, 1974).
	4. Always begin a conversation by thanking the other party for something they did for you "the other day" (Naotsuka, Sakamoto et al., 1981).
Saudi Arabians	1. Do not try to "get down to business" right away! Practice delivering polite inquiries, shaking hands for long periods of time, and offering coffee or tea before and after business negotiations (Harris & Moran, 1987).
	2. Practice overstating and exaggerating when making points (Adelman & Lustig, 1981; Prothro, 1955).
	3. Practice understanding the parallel constructions of logic used by speakers of Arabic (Adelman & Lustig, 1981; Kaplan, 1966).

TABLE 4.2
Intranational Dimension of Intercultural Behaviors

	Behaviors Anglo-Americans Can Adopt When Interacting With . . .
African Americans	1. Practice being more direct and open with the expression of feelings.
	2. Practice listening without interrupting.
	3. Practice demonstrating interest in black culture and perspectives (Items 1 through 3 from Kochman, 1981).
	4. Practice withholding value judgments when African Americans (males in particular) do not display such nonverbal gestures as making eye contact, nodding their heads, and saying *uh huh's* and *umm hmm's* during a conversation (Waters, 1990).
Hispanic Americans	1. Practice showing respect to those older than you. Hierarchy is considered very important by Puerto Rican Americans (Wurzel, 1983).
	2. Pay attention to their nonverbals and try adopting some of them. Try to understand what the gestures mean and how they are used (Collier, Ribeau, & Hecht, 1986).
	3. Practice sending verbal and nonverbal messages that you accept the person for who he or she is (Hecht & Ribeau, 1984).

children may be reinforced for shouting and slugging their siblings because their actions bring attention from their parents. It is thus assumed that to function well in a society these people must be taught more socially acceptable ways of interacting with others. Because the assumption is that they do not know *how,* the curriculum breaks down each skill into a simple step-by-step approach (Goldstein, 1988). To avoid oversimplification and de-contextualization, various topics for discussion are also included alongside the steps. The example in Table 4.3 provides a step-by-step coverage and trainer notes on how to apologize to someone in the United States.

Even those who display exceptional social skills within their own cultures are likely to feel awkward and unsure of themselves in another culture. These people have missed out on many of the "cultural secrets" that natives of that country have

TABLE 4.3
Apologizing

Steps to Follow	Trainer Notes
Step 1: Decide if you need to apologize for something you did.	Discuss how we sometimes do things for which we are later sorry. Apologizing is something we can do to let the other person know we are sorry. It also often makes us feel better.
Step 2: Think about your choices: a. Say it out loud to the person. b. Write the person a note.	Discuss when it is best to use verbal or written ways to apologize.
Step 3: Choose a good time and place.	Discuss how to choose a good time (apologize soon after the problem). The student may want to be alone with the person for a verbal apology.
Step 4: Carry out your best choice in a sincere way.	Discuss the body language and facial expression associated with sincerity. (Goldstein, 1988, p. 105)

learned through their socialization processes. Since many of these behaviors are taken for granted by adults and only taught to children, foreigners are rarely instructed on such basic social etiquette as the proper way to apologize, the proper way to ask a favor, and how to thank someone. The Skill-Streaming Approach thus appears to be a viable solution for teaching some of these prosocial skills. Although the original curriculum was written for the purpose of teaching prosocial skills as defined by American society, trainers with a good grasp of the concepts should be able to write their own culture-specific curriculum. Trainers can and should invite a resource person from the target culture to serve as a co-trainer. Although the basic ideas behind the approach will be covered in the following paragraphs, those who are interested in implementing the program should consult either *Skill-Streaming the Elementary School Child* (McGinnis, Goldstein, Sprafkin, & Gershaw, 1984) or *The Prepare Curriculum* (Goldstein, 1988).

The Skill-Streaming Approach attempts to replicate as closely as possible the natural learning process most people go through. For example, when learning a new skill such as playing baseball, the first thing we usually do is watch others. Once we have observed someone pitch the ball (modeling), we try pitching the ball ourselves in the privacy of our backyards (role-playing). We then ask supportive people around us (i.e., parents, siblings, friends) for their opinions and suggestions (performance feedback), practice the skill, and finally try the skill out on the baseball field (transfer of training). In the Skill-Streaming Approach, once the behavior is broken down into simple steps that can be followed, the trainer then proceeds with the same four steps: (1) modeling, (2) role-playing, (3) performance feedback, and (4) transfer of training (McGinnis et al., 1984).

MODELING

The trainer first discusses the step-by-step approach with the group, letting participants ask questions and make comments on various possible behaviors. Trainers should understand *why* the behavior is appropriate in the other culture. The trainer then conducts role-playing with a co-trainer and *models* the behavior step-by-step. The trainer should say the steps out loud while going through them the first time.

Several factors contribute to successful modeling. Trainers should make sure that they are going through the steps in order, that the steps are clear and detailed, that irrelevant material is excluded, and that they are repetitive enough to facilitate over-learning. Trainers should also rank-order the skills and start out with the easiest one; success is always a strong positive reinforcer. Models should rehearse specific role-playing enough so that trainees can gain credibility through their skillfulness in performing the behaviors. Learning is facilitated if at least one of the models is similar to the trainees' sociocultural background. Although it is crucial to have a resource person from the target culture demonstrate the behavior first, it is equally important for someone with a background similar to the group's to demonstrate the skill as well. This is to reinforce the fact that even foreigners can learn these behaviors if they try. Positive reinforcement is always very important. All role-playing should end with a successful outcome, thus reinforcing the behaviors.

ROLE-PLAYING

Once participants have observed the trainers model the behaviors they must then create their own vignettes to enact. *Role-playing* is most effective when trainees create situations that are relevant to their daily lives. Trainees are encouraged to make their scenes as real as possible by using various props and selecting people who closely resemble the actual characters in their scenario. Trainees are also encouraged to coach their collaborators on how best to portray the character (i.e., please speak in a deep voice, laugh a lot, be very moody). In the case of cross-cultural training sessions, however, the trainer might want to have at least one host-country national (more if possible) available to participate in the role-playing.

PERFORMANCE FEEDBACK

Immediately following role-playing, there should be a short feedback session. Its main purpose is to ensure that the trainee is performing the skill correctly and also to provide support and positive reinforcement. The coactors are first asked to comment on the trainee's performance. Before the role-playing begins, some of the observers are assigned to focus on a particular step. They are then asked to report on how well the trainee performed that particular skill. The other observers are then called on to provide overall feedback on the trainee's performance and give any suggestions on what can be done to further improve the trainee's skills. The trainers should then provide positive feedback and constructive criticism. Last, the main character is asked to evaluate and share with the others some comments and questions he or she may have. All trainees should have a chance to role-play the main character at least once for every new skill covered. For the more difficult skills, trainers are encouraged to have the participants role-play more than once.

TRANSFER OF TRAINING

Role-playing a behavior in a safe environment can be relatively simple. Implementing the behavior in a real-life situation, however, can be very difficult. Trainees are asked to do homework assignments between each session. They are asked to use the skill in an actual encounter with someone and to report on it later. There are at least three obvious benefits in assigning this task. The first is that trainees are more likely to try out the actual behavior in a real-life setting since they are given a specific time frame. The second is that trainees will receive immediate positive feedback during the following training session. Finally, if the trainees encounter problems or concerns regarding the particular skill, they can bring it up during the next training session.

◆ An Example: Jim's Case

Let us now turn back to the beginning of the chapter and reflect on the critical incident involving Jim. Although Jim was apparently very well-read in cross-cultural theories, he was unable to show sensitivity when faced with a Japanese student who used silence as a form of communication. Like many Americans, Jim reacted strongly to silence and grew uncomfortable very quickly. The first skill Jim must acquire is dealing with silence. Once he has mastered that skill, he might then move on to practicing the use of silence as a means of communication. Table 4.4 shows a sample plan of how this might be carried out using the Skill-Streaming Approach.

TABLE 4.4
Dealing With Silence

Steps to Follow	Trainer Notes
1. Take a deep breath and relax.	Discuss how Americans are uncomfortable with silence during a conversation. Ask the trainees why and talk about the cultural values that foster this belief.
2. Remind yourself that silence is not bad.	Discuss how silence is not necessarily bad in certain cultures. In Japan, for example, a pause is often used to mark respect or reverence.
3. Ask yourself what message this person is trying to convey through the silence. Is it respect? Or is it confusion? Is the person simply trying to say no? Or, does the person not understand what you are saying?	Discuss the various possible ways silence is used in Japan. Discuss how analyzing a situation can often be fun and can take our minds off our frustrations.
4. Think about the options. Should you repeat your question once more? Or, should you give the person some more time?	Also discuss tactful ways of approaching the situation if language is, in fact, the barrier.
5. Carry out your decision.	

Suggested Situations for Role-Plays:

1. You are an academic advisor for a Japanese student. She is not doing well in class and you need to come up with a strategy to improve her performance.

2. Your company is planning to market a few products to Japan. You have been sent to Japan for a week to make preliminary arrangements with the president of the company who will be doing the marketing for you.

3. You are hosting a foreign exchange student from Japan in your home. The student has told the director of the home-stay program that he is unhappy being forced to go to church every Sunday. You are hurt that he did not come to you directly.

As mentioned earlier, participants should be encouraged to create their own vignettes and make role-playing as real as possible to facilitate transfer of skills. Through combining Goldstein et al.'s Skill-Streaming Approach with culture-specific knowledge, trainers should be able to devise programs that provide trainees with specific behaviors to enhance communication with host-country nationals.

◆ Conclusion

The past few chapters have covered the basic content of a good cross-cultural training program (i.e., needs assessment, awareness, knowledge, emotions, and skills). We can thus assume that readers are ready to analyze how a good training curriculum covering these topics can be developed. The next chapter shows how to put everything together for the actual program. Although it is crucial that trainers spend sufficient time understanding these concepts and including them in their training curricula, they must also give due attention to the many logistical aspects that accompany the implementation of these programs. The following chapter discusses various issues that need to be addressed in making the final plans and arrangements for the "big day."

5

Putting the Elements Together

Designing and Administering an Effective Intercultural Training Program

◆ **Discussing the Possibilities of a Training Program**

Mary Carlson is the president of a small consulting firm that offers various types of services for businesses: training programs for newly promoted supervisors, motivational programs for salespeople, independent evaluations of the quality of programs offered by other firms, and so forth. One type of offering, and the type of work that is Mary Carlson's personal favorite, consists of various types of intercultural training programs. Fred Winthrop is a vice president of his city's First National Bank. He heard about Mary's work from a colleague he met because of his volunteer work with his city's symphony orchestra and opera. He called Mary Carlson long distance.

Fred: Is this Mary Carlson? I'm Fred Winthrop from First National Bank. Norm Oliver told me about some of your consulting work.

Mary: How is Norm? I enjoyed doing some program evaluation work with his company a few years ago.

Fred: He's fine. At First National, we're expanding into some overseas ventures, and Norm thought you may have some training programs that we could use.

Mary: What types of overseas ventures are you considering?

Fred: We'll probably be doing much more investing in businesses in Asia, and also in plants within the United States that have been recently bought by Asians. This will involve a great deal of contact with Asian businesspeople in a whole variety of ways, such as computer linkups, telephones, FAX machines, as well as personal visits.

Mary: Do you foresee any personnel from First National actually living in Asia for any length of time?

Fred: Yes, there might be 9 or 10 people who are given overseas assignments. What sorts of programs might we need?

Mary: If there is to be extensive intercultural contact, either taking place within this country or as part of an overseas assignment, I recommend a long-term program that includes treatments of cultural awareness, knowledge needed for effective communication, the emotional challenges intercultural communication can bring, and practice in specific behaviors that can increase the chances of effectiveness in your business negotiations. For people who might be assigned overseas, I also recommend that all family members be involved in training programs.

Fred: This sounds complex. How long would programs last?

Mary: I would propose week-long programs. I'd also propose that a person from my staff be allowed to spend about 3 days doing a needs assessment prior to the actual training. This will allow us to identify what intercultural experiences people have already had, what sorts of intercultural experiences they are ready for during training, what they would like to gain from the training programs, and what advice they have for the types of training methods that might be most acceptable to bank personnel.

Fred: This all sounds far more extensive than anything I had thought about. I was hoping that you could come in for a couple of hours and tell us about the basic "do's and don'ts." I thought you could tell us what we should do so that we don't get into so much trouble in our negotiations that we lose business!

During this telephone conversation, Fred Winthrop revealed an assumption about intercultural training that is widely shared.

Many people feel that the most important aspects of intercultural communication can be easily communicated in a few hours. In actuality, nothing could be further from the truth. Mary Carlson would probably prefer a training program that would run a full 2 weeks, but has undoubtedly learned from experience that businesses simply are unwilling to invest this amount of time. Further, she probably started with a proposal for a weeklong program, realizing that she might have to "bargain down" to a program that would last 3 days. In our experience, 3 days is the minimum time that combines a variety of concerns held by both trainers and clients. The first is the amount of money clients are willing to spend, which naturally increases with the length of a program. The second is the amount of time necessary to introduce basic ideas concerning cultural awareness, knowledge, emotional challenges, and behaviors. The third is the amount of time necessary for trainers to make a good impression such that they can bid for repeat business and make a case that training could be more effective with longer programs.

The purpose of this chapter is to describe some basic concerns in the design of a program. We will use the example of a 3-day program, even though we realize that this short amount of time will often be seen as a luxury by potential clients. The chapter covers three topic areas:

1. Designing a training program according to the four phases reviewed in Chapters 2, 3, and 4: awareness, knowledge, emotional challenges, and behavior. As part of our discussions, attention will also be given to trainee ethnocentrism and ethnorelativism (Chapter 3).
2. Some recommendations in case trainers are able to obtain contracts for longer programs (more than 3 days).
3. Practical concerns that must be kept in mind, such as staffing, working with difficult trainees, and adding flexibility to the program so as to respond to participants' specific needs.

To preview one of our pieces of advice, trainers must be extremely comfortable with the content and methods they choose for their programs. Observations of other trainers and extensive reading about content and methods are necessary, and many possibilities can be identified if these steps are taken. But just because someone else presents or writes about content and methods effectively, this should not be taken as an automatic recommendation for its adoption by other trainers. There must be the additional step during which trainers carefully answer the questions, "Am I comfortable with this content? Can I answer just about any question that trainees might have? Am I familiar enough with the training method, and can the reasons for using this method be vigorously defended?" We will be presenting methods and content from our own programs, and in many cases there are published references where far more detail is available. We realize, however, that many readers will not find this material suitable for their needs and so will not be able to use it. In many cases, this will be a wise decision if they can identify other content and methods with which they are more comfortable.

◆ **Decisions About Program Design**

Based on a needs assessment (Chapter 1), trainers should have good information about the amount of prior intercultural experience trainees have had, issues that trainees would like to see addressed, and advice concerning the types of methods that trainees will find acceptable. In our experience, many trainees in many types of organizations recognize that there is something called "culture" that influences behavior, and they are not embarrassed to admit that they need to know more about it.

◆ **Awareness**

In starting programs, then, we often introduce an awareness of "culture" by examining a list of its features that have been identified by anthropologists, psychologists, educators, and communication specialists. Described more fully in Brislin (1993), some of the features are:

1. Culture consists of concepts, values, and assumptions about life that guide behavior and that are widely shared by people. Discussions often center on examples of behaviors that culture guides (not directs absolutely), and examples of behaviors that people in a culture can expect of others given that the expectations are widely shared. If a male and female have a romantic relationship but decide not to marry, do they maintain a friendly relationship? Some cultures (e.g., Philippines) give guidance that is widely shared: they do not, because the maintenance of friendly relationships would be seen as threatening to current romances or marriages. Of course, there are exceptions, and this is a reminder that culture offers guidance that many people accept but that some will reject. Other cultures do not give much guidance (e.g., middle-class United States), and so final decisions are based on individual differences. Some Americans maintain relationships with former romantic partners, and other choose not to. Understanding the difference between cultural guidance and individual differences is an important step within the awareness stage of training.

2. Culture consists of ideas that are transmitted generation to generation, rarely with explicit instruction, by parents, teachers, religious figures, and other respected elders. This means that there will be identifiable childhood experiences that lead to the transmission of culture. A good exercise is to ask participants, "What are some childhood experiences with which many people from your cultural background will be familiar? Did these experiences lead to the transmission of cultural values?" For example, the concept "power distance" was introduced in Chapter 4. In high power distance cultures, people accept and are satisfied with the fact that some individuals have far more status and authority than do others. Further, these high-status people can expect as their right that they will receive deference and respect from others. In schools, this means that teachers

receive a great deal of respect. In the workplace, this means that the directives of bosses are followed. People from low power distance countries (e.g., the United States) may remember the childhood experience where their parents argued with a teacher about an aspect of a child's classroom behavior during a parent-teacher conference. The childhood experience may have involved a child and his or her parents taking the same side and trying to put a teacher on the defensive. This type of experience would occur far less frequently in a high power distance country. There, the teacher and parent would join forces and put pressures on the child to do better! In a training program for American businesspeople about to take assignments in high power distance countries (e.g., many in Asia), these examples of childhood experiences lead to helpful discussions about supervisor-subordinate relations (Brislin, 1993).

3. Culture becomes clearest when people interact with others from very different backgrounds. Culture becomes clear in "well-meaning clashes." People are engaging in proper behavior according to their own culture, but there is a clash when the interaction is between people from different cultural backgrounds. There is no "right way" or "wrong way" in these interactions. Rather, the backgrounds of people must be understood to determine what guidance their cultures have given them.

Some of the clearest examples stem from people's socialization in an individualistic culture in contrast to a collectivist culture (as introduced in Chapter 4). When people from different cultures meet for the first time, who might communicate a sense of excitement and dynamism and who might communicate a sense of dullness and/or wariness? People from individualist countries such as the United States very often develop a dynamic style because they want to communicate their abilities and uniqueness when they meet others. They do not have a supportive collective that takes on this task: individualists have to do it themselves! In contrast, people from many collective cultures (e.g., India) have a supportive group whose members take on the task of extolling the talents of any one member. Any one person, then, does not have to behave in a dynamic and memorable style when meeting others for the first time. In addition, a collectivist may communicate a sense of wariness when meeting others since she or he does not know if the others will be helpful or harmful to the collective. After a number of interactions, collectivists may "warm up" to the others, and these newcomers can take the gradually increasing warmth as a sign that the collective (not just any one person) is offering a certain amount of acceptance.

As part of the discussions concerning these features of culture (12 are discussed in Brislin, 1993), trainers can draw upon the experiences of the more interculturally experienced trainees. Keep in mind that we are assuming that ethnorelative trainees (or trainees ready for the move to ethnorelativism) will be identified as part of the needs assessment. Because the discussion topics (widely shared experiences, childhood experiences, clashes) can generate many examples from trainees, our experience has been that ethnocentric trainees can slowly begin to contribute to the discussions. An especially good indicator of any move toward ethnorelativism takes place when trainees begin to discuss cultural differences, such as behaviors influenced by individualism and collectivism, in a nonjudgmental way. If they show an understanding that a dynamic self-presentation style is not "good" in and of itself, and that a more modest style may be more suitable in some parts of the world, then they are showing an understanding of cultural relativism.

◆ Knowledge

After trainees become *aware* of culture's influence on behavior, programs can then deal with knowledge useful in intercultural interactions and in adjustment to other cultures. In our experience, the use of critical incidents has a number of benefits. Critical incidents consist of short stories that involve the interaction of people from different cultures. Incidents have characters with names, a plot line, and an ending that involves some sort of problem and/or misunderstanding. In analyzing reasons for the problems and misunderstandings, trainees begin to learn about culturally influenced knowledge that can have major impacts on people's intercultural interactions.

We have found critical incidents so useful that we have created a set of them to introduce the chapters in this book. Using these incidents as examples, trainees would be asked to give reasons for the intercultural difficulties and to suggest the types of knowledge necessary to prevent the problems from ever occurring. In the incident involving Fakir from India (Chapter 1), analysis would center on the knowledge he needs to make normal progress toward his graduate degree. There are important facts that underlie Fakir's problems: In his home country, graduate students wait for direction concerning research topics from their professors. In the United States, professors expect students to take a great deal of initiative. In the incident involving Mark and Susan and their work with newly arrived immigrants (Chapter 2), an important piece of information is that immigrants often find the behavior of Americans fickle and superficial. Mark and Susan should become aware of their tendency to give less attention to reasonably well-settled immigrants in their quest to help others who have arrived within the past week. In the incident involving Karen, the wife of an executive who has been assigned to the presidency of his corporation's branch in Mexico (Chapter 3), the often-neglected fact is that accompanying spouses often have no clear role and consequently no outlet for their talents. Attention to ways in which accompanying spouses can integrate themselves in the host culture so that they have a sense of purpose is a high-priority topic for discussion.

In using critical incidents, trainees should be introduced to the concept that knowledge about different behaviors is central to success in intercultural encounters. During discussions that raise their level of knowledge, then, trainees may begin to think about the desirability of changing certain behaviors (the final phase in training, to be discussed later in this chapter). Brislin and his colleagues (1986) created a collection of 100 critical incidents that have been widely used in training programs. Here is an example of an incident that generates good discussions of the knowledge necessary for successful intercultural encounters as well as the possibility of behavior change. The incident is called "The Proposal Process" (Brislin et al., 1986, pp. 151-152: number 55 in the collection of 100 incidents).

Called to a staff meeting by his principal, Stan Brown from New Zealand reread materials on a mathematics curriculum development project that he wished to see incorporated into the high school at which he taught. Stan had been teaching in the Philippines for 2 years and was enjoying his sojourn at an international school in Manila that attracted not only Filipino students but also students from many other countries whose parents worked in the Philippines.

José, who had developed a close relationship with Stan, was also asked to the meeting. The principal asked Stan to review his proposal, the substance of which was already know to the others at the meeting. The proposal went through without very much modification and it was agreed to take the next step toward possible, eventual implementation. Because this had taken less time than expected, the principal asked José to say a few words about another curriculum development project on which he (José) was working. Again, most of the people at the meeting knew of this project. José gave an outline of his thinking, and Stan then asked some difficult questions that forced José to think quickly on his feet and to defend some of his earlier assumptions. The principal called an end to the meeting, and José then told Stan that he could not meet for dinner as earlier planned. Stan was puzzled by José's cancellation because José seemed upset when informing Stan of his wish not to meet for dinner.

Of these four alternatives, which gives an insight into the reasons for José's cancellation of the dinner appointment?

1. José wanted to go to a library to get more information so as to better defend his proposal in the future.
2. José was jealous that Stan's proposal had passed on to the next step toward implementation without very much modification.
3. José felt that Stan withdrew his friendship at the meeting.

4. The principal asked José to sharpen up his thinking about his proposal.

Most groups of trainees are able to identify Alternative 3 as the most helpful in analyzing reasons for the difficulties presented in this incident. Trainers can further guide participants to an understanding of the culturally based reasons for the difficulties. Some of the reasons relate to the discussion of individualism and collectivism as introduced in Chapter 4. Stan is an individualist, and so he speaks up and makes his personal opinions known. José is a collectivist who has developed a close relationship with Stan, and in so doing has undoubtedly begun to make overtures toward including Stan in his collective. Harmony is important in collectives, and members do not do anything that might cause embarrassment (often referred to as loss of face).

Discussions can also center on the possibility of behavior change. People might suggest that Stan learn to behave according to the guidance that collectivist cultures suggest. Stan can certainly make suggestions to José, but they should be made in private. Brislin and his colleagues (1986) added:

> Even here, however, Stan would want to be sure that he is making his suggestions in [an acceptable style]. The style would include saying a number of good things about the proposal, being much more indirect than he would in his own country, and keeping the tone of the meeting light with jokes and anecdotes. (p. 173)

When covering the knowledge necessary for effective intercultural communication, and when using critical incidents, ethnocentric trainees often begin to rebel. A typical reaction will be: "Why should Stan change his behavior? All people who make proposals should learn to accept criticism and to 'take it.' You trainers have said that there will be a lot more contact among people from different parts of the world. People like José better learn to accept criticism in public forums!" We want to add that not all people who make comments such as these are ethnocentric. People can also make such comments from an ethnorelative perspective if they add remarks such as, "I'm afraid that if Stan modifies his behavior, José will not learn to deal with criticism from other individualists who may be far more vigorous and possibly far more obnoxious than Stan." The keys to recognizing ethnocentrism are that (a) no recognition is given to the fact that people in the critical incidents have points of view influenced by their culture, and (b) there is no evidence of any sympathy or empathy concerning the reactions of people from cultural backgrounds other than the trainee's. Our advice to dealing with ethnocentric reactions is to turn the issue over to the training group as a whole. Trainers might say, "A number of views have been expressed concerning this incident. Do people have any reactions to views other than their own? Is there any consensus concerning what Stan or José might do in the future?" There will be continued ill feelings on the part of the most ethnocentric trainees, but there is the possibility that these reactions will be dissipated across all the people involved in the training program and not directed just at the trainers. Further (and assuming that the ethnorelative participants put their views forward clearly), the ethnocentric trainees learn that some of their peers have different views. Over time, and probably long after the program, these different and more ethnorelative views may grow given the "seeding" that took place during the training program.

◆ Emotional Challenges

As has undoubtedly become clear, there are no hard and fast boundaries among the phases of training that we are discussing. Examples of cultural awareness inevitably introduce differences in what is considered appropriate knowledge that members of a culture should possess. We have already discussed the fact that treatments of knowledge introduce behaviors that people can consider modifying. When people are exposed to knowledge differences, they can have intense emotional reactions. People spend a great deal of time and energy learning what their culture considers to be appropriate knowledge concerning how best to interact with others, how best to interview for jobs, and so forth. It is upsetting to discover that people from other cultures have very different views concerning appropriate knowledge.

When dealing with the subject of emotional challenges more directly, we have found two methods especially useful. One is the use of critical incidents that generate discussions concerning the characters' emotional reactions, and the second is the use of prepared and scripted role-playing. In many cases, the same set of materials can be used for both approaches. Critical incidents can be discussed, and then the critical incidents can form the basis of prepared and scripted role-playing. For example, the following incident was created by Teresa Takaki as part of efforts to develop materials for health care workers. It is called "The Crowded Office" (Brislin & Takaki, 1992, pp. 72-74).

A young Hawaiian girl was diagnosed as having leukemia. Her parents went along with any decisions the physician made. At one point, the girl's physician thought it would be a good time to ask the family to come in for another consultation. When they came they brought the whole extended family with them as well as close friends. The physician found 34 people waiting at his office.

The office was small and could not hold everyone. The physician told the girl's parents that only the immediate family would be needed. The parents and especially the grandparents became insistent on having the whole family present; at least the cousins, aunts, and uncles should talk with the doctor. The physician was trying to convince the parents that it would be impossible and that only the immediate family was necessary. The grandparents became angry. They couldn't understand the reason for the doctor's request.

The physician told the group that he would talk to only the parents that day. The parents instead left and later changed their daughter's physician.

How would you explain the family's behavior?

1. The Hawaiians, reflecting their culture, were curious and could be considered "nosy." The extended family and friends wanted to know what the physician was going to say.
2. The family did not trust the doctor. He hadn't cured her yet and he didn't spend enough time with her.
3. The Hawaiians are a close collective society. It is the group that is responsible for the girl so they all came to the doctor's office.
4. There was no significant reason why the extended family and friends came to the appointments.

If they have been exposed to basic ideas about individualism and collectivism, participants are able to choose Alternative 3. Discussions can center on the emotional reactions of the different people. The physician will be upset because he does not know how to deal with the number of people in his office. The family members will be upset because the physician seems so insensitive. Trainers can guide the discussions so that program participants identify the reasons for emotional reactions given the backgrounds of the different people. The physician is concerned with such issues as the use of his time (he has other patients), diseases that might be transmitted given the density of people in his office, and the confidentiality of his patient's records. The family members feel that because all of them are responsible for the well-being of the patient, they should all be informed. Further, they will be upset that traditional status distinctions (the role of the grandparents) are being ignored. Another point that trainers might introduce is that although there may occasionally be acceptable compromises, such as meetings with the entire family in a hospital auditorium, there often will not. Many times, the contribution to be made by a knowledge of intercultural communication is the identification of underlying reasons for misunderstandings. Misunderstandings will occur. People become especially upset, and experience great stress, if they have no idea why problems have occurred. There are at least two reasons for their stress: (1) not knowing why people are behaving as they are and (2) not being able to do anything about it. If they understand some of the underlying reasons, such as the individualistic versus collectivistic socialization of people, they will experience a decrease in the stress due to the first reason. There are other benefits. If people understand culturally based reasons for behavior, they are less likely to make negative attributions (Chapter 2) about individuals from other cultures. Further, if people understand underlying reasons and can use relatively neutral terms, such as *individualism* and *collectivism,* they will more likely have productive discussions during which possible compromises and/or behavioral plans (Chapter 4) can be formulated.

Another method trainers can use to introduce emotional confrontations is "scripted role-playing." We are using the term *scripted* to summarize our recommendation that role-playing be carefully planned. Trainers might start with critical incidents because many have the basic elements of role-playing scenarios that trainees can develop. Consider one of the examples in this chapter. In the incident involving Stan, José, and the proposal, trainers would ask for volunteers who would play the various parts. One trainee would play Stan, another would play José, another would play the principal, and so forth. Trainees would meet and would decide how they will play out the incident. In our experience, 20 to 30 minutes is enough for this planning process. Trainees decide who will start the incident, what general sorts of things will be said in the dialogue, key transition points (e.g., "When I say this, then you walk out of the meeting!"), and the verbalization or behavior that will end the role-playing. The trainees would then play out their scenario for the entire training group. During the time this group is planning their role-playing, another group can be developing another critical incident (e.g., the doctor and the family) for role-playing. This other group later plays out this scenario for all the other workshop participants.

From our experience, we have some pieces of advice for the use of role-playing. Most important, role-playing should only be used when trainers and trainees are comfortable with each other and have developed trust. Given that we have assumed that there will be a needs assessment involving trainer-trainee interaction during which people can begin the acquaintance process, our experience has been that role-playing can be introduced during the second half of the second day of training. By that time, trainers will have been able to demonstrate their knowledge, show their concern for trainees, and demonstrate that they will not abuse their power. Role-playing involves risks: trainees are volunteering to stand up in front of their colleagues and perhaps look silly. Another piece of advice stems from our use of the term *scripted role-playing.* Trainees should be able to prepare their scenarios and be comfortable when they actually play them out in front of the entire workshop. Trainers should be firm in establishing the rule, "no surprises." Once trainees agree to the general scenario, they must abide by the rule and avoid making changes during the actual role-playing. Problems with the use of role-playing (Brislin & Pedersen, 1976; Gudykunst & Hammer, 1983) occur when trainees have to react to unexpected events. Often, they become uncomfortable, feel threatened, and sometimes lose control over their emotions. Because they are doing this in front of their peers, they become especially upset and embarrassed. One reason unexpected events occur is that a trainee, at the last second, decides to add something to the role-playing "just to see how others will react." This last-minute addition may be the sort of unexpected event that causes a severe emotional reaction. One of us remembers a training session in which role-playing was used.

The scenario involved male-female interactions in the workplace. The trainees met to develop their scenario, but the no-surprises rule had not been introduced strongly enough. During the actual role-playing in front of all workshop participants, one of the male trainees added a new behavior at the last minute just to see what would happen. The behavior happened to remind one of the female participants of the rapist who had attacked her 2 years earlier. She lost control of her emotions, and the entire training program came to a halt. The rest of the day was spent dealing with her emotions, and she was not able to finish the workshop the next day. Role-playing is a powerful and potentially effective tool, but it also is easy to misuse. If trainers keep in mind the recommendations to use role-playing only after trust is established and if they also emphasize the reasons for the no-surprises rule, we believe that it is a method worthy of careful consideration.

◆ Behavior

Our strong recommendation is that, whenever possible, trainers guide workshop participants in carrying out specific behaviors that will increase their chances of intercultural success. Further, trainers should introduce the exact reasons for the recommendation that certain behaviors be adopted. Some examples have already been given. Foreign students from Asia (the incident that introduced Chapter 1) could practice developing a list of research ideas that they would present to a professor. This could be done as part of scripted role-playing, with either the trainer or another participant playing the professor. In the incident involving the American couple and their work with recent immigrants (introduction in Chapter 2), trainees could practice behaviors that lead to the maintenance of interpersonal relations. These can include stopping by for visits to just eat and chat, not necessarily to deal with some problem that has arisen. In the incident involving the physician and the extended family, health professionals could practice such behaviors as identifying high-status people and communicating through them, addressing large groups and at the same time making everyone feel personally involved, and enlisting the support of the collective in any long-term medical treatment.

We are not claiming that the introduction of behaviors that people might change is an easy task. People become accustomed to very specific actions and find it hard to break habitual ways of behaving. As part of his interviews for his book, *A World of Ideas,* Bill Moyers (1990, p. 195) asked: "What would be the one thing I'd like to have settled for myself? And it is this. Why is it that I can't change my ways?" One answer to Moyers's question is that behaving in certain ways has proven beneficial to people in the past. Given these past successes,

Telephone: (214) 928-4917
Peter Reed
Sales and Marketing
Member:
Sierra Club
New Orleans Jazz Society
(Printed on recycled paper)

Figure 5.1. Sample Business Card

people do not see any need to change. This observation allows us to reiterate our recommendation. When suggesting changes, trainers must give people exact reasons for adopting the new behaviors. People are likely to entertain change only when they understand that the new behaviors will lead to a greater probability of success during their interactions with culturally different others.

We also recommend that the first behavior that trainers introduce be nonthreatening and relatively easy to carry out. In programs for business people about to travel to Asia, the preparation of business cards is a good example. As an exercise, trainees might be asked to create a business card that they would be comfortable using in their own country. For example, a trainee from the United States might create the card shown in Figure 5.1.

When asked why, the trainee might say that the card emphasizes some of his personal interests. But would the card be useful in Asia? Would it lead to success in the form of help obtaining appointments with important businesspeople? The answer is "no." The card emphasizes Peter's individual interests but does not fit him into a collective. The card does not indicate Peter's place within the hierarchy of his organization. In some Asian languages (e.g., Japanese), speakers must choose among various levels of speech according to people's status. If Japanese businesspeople do not know the status represented by the other person's title, then they literally do not know how to

BARNSWORTH MANUFACTURING
Peter Reed
Vice President, Sales and Marketing
Telephone: (214) 928-4917
Fax: (214) 928-4740
Bitnet: REED@Barnsworth

Figure 5.2. Sample Business Card

speak to the person. As one of us was told prior to his first speaking tour in Japan, "If people don't know your status within your organization, they will not know who you are!" After this discussion, trainees can be asked to prepare another card that will be useful to them in Asia. They might develop something like that in Figure 5.2. Trainers can use the results of this short exercise to emphasize the basic point that changes in behavior can increase the chances of success.

Once this safe and nonthreatening example is introduced, trainers can move to more sensitive behaviors. In a program for people about to live in Japan, the need to understand the necessity of thanking others can be covered. In the same way that Americans greet people with "Hi! How are you?" the Japanese often greet each other with *"Kono aida wa domo arigato gozai-mashita"* (Thank you for your past favor). The concept of thanking someone instead of saying "How are you?" is an alien concept to many foreigners. Because one must always thank the other person for something that occurred during their previous encounter, the favor can actually refer to something that occurred more than a year ago, as long as that was the last encounter with that particular person. Many foreigners find themselves at a loss when their Japanese friends thank them for something that occurred many years before. Given that they may never have developed the habit, even sojourners who reside in Japan and speak the language fluently customarily forget to use this phrase when greeting their friends or acquaintances. Naotsuka and Sakamoto (1981) discussed the case of an American woman who found herself forgetting to use the phrase even after residing in Japan for more than 18 years. Omission of this phrase can not only "throw the other person off" but is often interpreted as a lack of appreciation of the other person's generosity. Foreigners may find their Japanese counterparts worried that they (the foreigners) did not enjoy the dinner, the gift, the conversation, or whatever may have occurred during their last encounter and thus make many inquiries about what displeased them. Making a habit of saying *"kono aida wa domo arigato gozaimashita"* not only facilitates the conversation but is an effective means of conveying one's appreciation of others.

The fact that the American woman mentioned earlier has difficulty remembering to use the phrase even after living in Japan for 18 years reinforces the idea that knowledge alone is not enough to instill specific behaviors. Practicing the phrase through role-playing should be an easy yet effective way to master this skill. Trainers must, however, expect some resistance from trainees who feel that this custom is superficial and even fake. Trainers may want to remind those people that many foreigners find the American greeting of "How are you?" as being equally shallow because an accurate summary of one's current feelings is not appropriate. It is therefore crucial that trainees understand why, where, when, and how the phrase should be used before actually practicing the behaviors. For those that do not speak Japanese and find that the phrase "Thank you for the other day" sounds awkward, creating set phrases to suit different occasions and memorizing them should prove to be an effective substitute. Table 5.1 lists suggested phrases that trainees may want to practice using. Trainees are encouraged to create their own phrases because it is crucial that the greeting appear smooth and natural.

FINISHING THE PROGRAM

After encouraging trainees to identify and to practice actual behaviors, our recommendation is to reserve approximately 1½ hours for a final workshop summary and question-answer

TABLE 5.1
Socially Appropriate Phrases Showing Thanks
for Past Activities in Japan

Activity Last Shared	Phrase
Dinner	Mr. or Mrs. _____, thank you very much for a lovely dinner last night/ week/month!
Conversation	Mr. or Mrs. _____, thank you so much for taking the time to come and see me last night/week/month!
Receiving a gift	Mr. or Mrs. _____, thank you for such a thoughtful gift. I really enjoyed it!

session. A good way to organize the summary is to reiterate the four-part structure of the workshop and to list concepts and examples that were covered during discussions of each part. This suggestion is based on the assumption that someone on the program staff will keep careful notes of concepts that were covered and participants' own examples and/or expansions of the concepts. The training director would provide a copy of the notes for each participant and would use the notes as the outline for his or her summary presentation. For example, in the notes on "Awareness," a concept listed might be "childhood experiences that instill cultural values." Next to that listing, the notes might read: "John's (one of the participants) example of having a morning paper route that introduced him to the importance of the work ethic." Under the notes for "Behavior," the concept might be "modifications that clearly proved more effective." Next to this listing, the notes might read: "Elizabeth's example of working with a Hispanic employee and finding it much more effective to make suggestions for improvement in private rather than in public."

There are a number of advantages to a summary presentation based on this type of notes. The procedure allows the trainers to show their interest in the unique experiences of participants and the unique needs of their organization, because the notes would clearly not be the same as those prepared after a workshop given in another organization. The notes also should appeal to the memories of the participants because it is their examples and expansions that are being included. If the notes clearly indicate that a great deal of material has been covered, it would be appropriate for trainers to list topics that might be covered in future workshops. In taking this step, the trainers would begin their lobbying for "repeat business" from the same company. In our experience, if trainers are to make a living offering workshops, they must attract repeat business.

◆ **Longer Programs**

At times, trainers will be permitted to organize programs that will run longer than 3 days. Our recommendation for longer programs is that (a) trainees be introduced to various behaviors that they will be asked to perform in other cultures, and that (b) these behaviors be performed in social contexts similar to those that will be experienced in the host culture. We assume that, at the end of 3 days, that trainers and trainees will have learned to trust each other and that trainees will be willing to take risks performing unfamiliar behaviors. One reason for this willingness is that they are convinced that trainers would not ask them to perform behaviors that are unreasonable. Rather, trainees will be confident that the behaviors called for will assist in their successful adjustment to the other culture.

There are models of long-term programs that have emphasized the introduction of behaviors in various social contexts. To prepare for this type of program, trainers ask and answer this question: "What behaviors will be called for in the other culture, and where/when/why will these behaviors be appropriate?" The work of Trifonovitch (1977) has already been reviewed. To prepare Peace Corps volunteers and contract teachers for life in rural Pacific Island societies, Trifonovitch created a simulated village during training. There, trainees had to gather and cook their own food, make their own entertainment, provide for the disposal of waste materials, learn to tell time by observing the sun and tides, and so forth. Trifonovitch argued that these behaviors would be necessary for success in everyday life and that they could be rehearsed during training. To prepare Anglo (called *Pakeha* in New Zealand) counselors to interact effectively with Maoris in New Zealand, a 3-day program involving extensive Pakeha-Maori contact was organized (Everts, 1988). This unique 3-day program took place after preliminary training sessions during which trainees and Maori advisers became acquainted with each other. All interactions and adoptions of new behaviors took place in a tribal village where Maori norms and customs guided the efforts of trainees over the 3-day period. For example, "Under the guidance of craft experts, trainees participated in restoring or developing Maori community facilities. Experts and tribal elders also explained traditional Maori strategies of promoting mental, spiritual and social welfare" (Everts, 1988, pp. 99-100). Trainees also learned that in Maori meetings, time is treated in a more leisurely manner than in New Zealand cities. "Anyone has the right to speak as they wish, that strong customs pertain regarding gracious courtesy and respect, and that decisions are made by communal consensus" (Everts, 1988, p. 100).

As another example of long-term training involving behaviors, Goodnow (1992) described programs offered for adolescents who volunteer to work with Amigos de las Americas. The "Amigos" organization attracts adolescents who want to spend their summers working in community health projects in Latin American countries. In designing training programs, administrators have clearly kept in mind the experiences that young North Americans will face in Latin American villages. During training, volunteers spent long hours digging latrines during a downpour, had their passports stolen, walked from place to place with only a rough map to guide them, and slept in straw because their sleeping bags were misplaced somewhere. As part of their training, "Spanish speaking exchange students, posing as provocateurs, . . . challenge [the trainees] with every mishap that could befall them in their host country" (Goodnow,

1992, p. C1). There will probably be more dropouts during this type of intense training than in the milder forms described elsewhere in this book. Trainers must foresee this possibility and must discuss it with the sponsoring organization. One defense of intense training involving behaviors is that some people can learn, during training, that they will not benefit from (and will not be able to make contributions to) the type of cross-cultural experience they had been anticipating. It is much less stressful, and much less expensive to the sponsoring organization, if this fact is learned during training rather than during the actual assignment.

We realize that given practical considerations of time and space, many uses of the "behaviors in context" approach will be more limited in scope than the three examples reviewed here. Our recommendation is that trainees call upon their creativity and use the examples as stimuli for their thinking. For example, assume that trainers have access to a room that is 50 feet long and 30 feet wide. This room would be large enough to break into three sections where different behaviors could be practiced. In a program for international students, different sections could be used for extensive role-playing involving registering for courses, one-on-one sessions with faculty advisers, and participation in small seminars with other students.

In a program for international business in Japan, one section could be labeled "entrance," and various greetings and business-card exchanges could take place. Another section could be used for the one-on-one negotiations necessary to introduce a potential joint-venture agreement. The third section could be used for the group meeting where the agreement (whose details have already been hammered out) is announced [as described in Brislin et al. (1986, pp. 182, 270) as part of their discussion of decision making in Japan]. In a program for technical assistance advisers, one part of the room could be devoted to interactions between advisers and various "stakeholders" who have an interest in the success (and sometimes the failure) of a project. Another part of the room could be used for interviews as part of the selection process for project personnel, and the third part could be used for interactions that center on the transfer of skills from advisers to hosts. Skill transfer is central to the long-term success of projects, and advisers who integrate skill transfer into their jobs increase the chances of their own intercultural effectiveness (Hawes & Kealey, 1981).

◆ Practical Issues That Have Been Identified by Experienced Trainers

Whenever they gather together at professional meetings, experienced trainers often share their recent successes as well as their efforts that led to some difficulties. Their reports often contain very good information that can be considered by others. The following items are frequently discussed (see also Ptak, Cooper, & Brislin, 1994, for a report on the recommendations of experienced trainers).

LETTING TRAINEES INDIVIDUATE THEMSELVES

Especially in short programs where there is a great deal of material to cover, trainers often want to begin their coverage of intercultural communication issues quickly. This can be a mistake! Very often, trainees who find themselves in an intercultural workshop have already had some relevant experiences and/or have accomplished a great deal in their lives. They want to be recognized as individuals, not as nearly anonymous people in a workshop. At times, they will want to make contributions to which their name is attached. Trainers should be sensitive to this need for recognition, and an easy way to address the issue is to encourage trainees to talk about themselves. In fact, this can be the first major activity of the workshop. After trainers introduce themselves and present an overview of the workshop, they can "go around the table" and ask trainees to present some key information about themselves. This can include their names, current positions, previous intercultural experience, and any hopes they have for the workshop. Trainers who have developed the skill of remembering names will be rewarded if they can later call upon participants and ask them to expand upon a certain point based on information gathered during these self-introductions. Even though trainers might feel that a set of self-introductions is not a good use of time, they are wrong! If people do not feel individualized, they will often become very rebellious and make life miserable for members of the training staff. One of us remembers a very unsuccessful program. The reason stemmed from the lack of opportunities for trainees to call attention to themselves as unique individuals. Their frustration eventually escalated to a point where the trainees tried to take over administration of the program. They argued that they knew as much or more than the training staff and that their potential contributions had not been recognized and integrated into the program.

FLEXIBILITY

The issue of trainee rebelliousness leads to a discussion of flexibility. Before they decide on a full-scale rebellion, participants almost always make suggestions for modifications in the program. Trainers are wise to address as many of these as possible. When trainers prepare a full schedule for their workshop, they must realize that modifications will often be necessary. Often, the need for modifications will become clear during the self-introductions discussed in the previous section. Even with an excellent needs assessment, last minute changes bring about the need for program modification. For example, people who were interviewed as part of a needs assessment might have experienced changes in their lives that prevent their attendance at the actual program. Their substitutes may have different needs based on their jobs, their past experiences, their readiness for participation in experiential training, and so forth. Examples of changes include more role-playing and fewer lectures, critical incidents that involve elements very similar to aspects of the participants' lives, and increased time for group discussions where trainees can share their insights. Trainers who are flexible and who can make program modifications will reap many benefits. Participants will be appreciative when they see that their suggestions are clearly part of the revised schedule of activities. Participants will also make positive conclusions about any trainer who obviously has such extensive knowledge about both content and methods that he or she can make quick modifications. These positive attributions should contribute to the likelihood of repeat business.

DEALING WITH THE CONCEPT OF STEREOTYPES EARLY

Any discussions of culture's effects on communication inevitably include several generalizations. A number have been covered throughout this book: Asian students often wait for their advisers to direct the choice of research topics, Filipinos become upset when friends disagree with them in public, and so forth. In virtually all programs with which we have been involved, a trainee will complain, "Aren't these just stereotypes of people from different cultures?" Given the frequency of comments about stereotypes, we recommend that trainers discuss the concept early in training. Trainers might write down a number of concepts on a chalkboard: culture provides guidance to behavior, stereotypes, generalizations backed by research, and individual differences. Trainers can then explain that we must make generalizations about behavior, but that the difference between reasonable generalizations and stereotypes is that the former are backed by research, are consciously held, and allow for individual differences (Adler, 1991). If the different concepts are introduced, trainers can say, "When I say that the Japanese are very sensitive to people's position in their hierarchy within their organizations, I am making a generalization" (point to term on board). "However, I am also keeping in mind that there will be individual differences: Sojourners in Japan will encounter hosts whose business cards do not include their position in a hierarchy" (point to the term "individual differences" on the board). When trainers introduce generalizations, stereotypes, and individual differences and encourage participants to make distinctions among them, complaints are less likely to arise. Possible complaints have been defused by the trainer's willingness to discuss "problems brought on by stereotypes" in a direct manner.

THE "TEN PERCENT FACTOR"

The issues of rebelliousness, the need for flexibility, and the coverage of controversial topics such as stereotypes bring up another basic point. No matter how good the needs assessment and how careful the planning, approximately 10% of trainees will disapprove of the training staff's choices regarding method and content. When trainers meet to compare notes, they often refer to this as "the 10% factor" and also make additional and related observations. For example, one experienced trainer (in Ptak et al., 1994) added that 10% will not merely dislike the content, they will also not like the training staff! There are many reasons for the 10% factor. Some trainees genuinely want either more or less active learning exercises. If they want more, trainees complain, "The staff is not taking advantage of the expertise possessed by the participants." If they want less, trainees complain, "My company is paying to bring in experts to give us the most advanced knowledge, and the staff is responding by asking far less experienced trainees (like myself) to make contributions." Trainers obviously have to work hard to balance the demands of trainees who want more and less participation, but whatever the decision some participants will conclude that the staff erred in emphasizing the wrong direction along the more-less dimension.

Other reasons for the 10% factor include personality clashes among trainers and trainees, trainee resistance in moving from ethnocentrism to ethnorelativism (Chapter 2), and trainee self-assessments of their own expertise. There is a strange phenomenon in intercultural communication: some people who have done a little (e.g., they have had a few interactions with international students on an American university campus) conclude that they are experts whose attendance at workshops is unnecessary. They feel that they are more knowledgeable than the trainers and are upset upon discovering that they will not be treated in a special manner that clearly distinguishes them from other participants. Dealing with such participants is one of the skills trainers have to learn if they are to be successful.

STAFFING DECISIONS

Any discussion of trainer skills quickly leads to discussions concerning the selection of staff members for a program. Especially in longer programs, budgets should be prepared that allow the contributions of several staff members. We realize that this will not always be possible given the lack of willingness of many organizations to fund programs adequately, but a discussion of multiple staff members at least allows trainers to consider targets toward which they can work as their careers develop.

No matter how skillful any one trainer is, there have to be limits to the number of presentations he or she should make. If there is only one trainer, participants get tired of looking at him or her after about 2 days. In addition to making a few presentations, other trainers should be selected with the need for additional skills in mind. At times, one person may have several of the following desiderata. One staff member should be extremely knowledgeable, through extensive reading and hands-on experience, about both content and methods in intercultural communication. This is the person who will be able to make recommendations upon hearing trainee requests for modifications in the planned program and who will make many of the formal presentations. Another person, who has a reputation of being socially adept, should be very skillful in working with trainees who complain a lot. This person should be good at listening carefully, offering condolences, and communicating that as much as is humanly possible will be done to handle the complaints. One image of this person is that he or she is similar to the airline employee who patiently handles complaints of lost baggage at 2:00 A.M. when passengers want to go home or go to their hotels. If the extremely knowledgeable person is not skillful at fielding questions from trainees, the socially skilled person can take on this task. We have observed trainers who are so knowledgeable that they become impatient when participants ask very basic, simple questions. If this could be a problem, trainers should have enough self-insight to pass on tasks to others who are more skillful at handling specific aspects of the program.

Still another staff member should be immediately credible to trainees because of job experiences or obvious expertise in the content or cultures under consideration. For example, in a program preparing Canadian businesspeople for assignments in Germany, an ideal staff member would be either a German national or a Canadian who has clearly experienced business successes in Germany. These people do not have to be experts in the broad concerns of intercultural communication training, but they should be able to give specific examples of concepts that other trainers introduce (e.g., specific stereotypes, specific examples of work norms and corporate culture as discussed in Chapter 2). Both of us were recently involved in a workshop dealing with cultural differences in the delivery of health services. A good deal of time and energy had to be spent on this question: "We are health professionals: physicians, nurses, and public health workers. Why should we listen to you?" One reason we could deal with the question is that some of our training materials had been generated in collaboration with health professionals, and some of the guest presenters in the workshop were physicians and professors in schools of public health.

Another staff member should be very skillful in the administrative aspects surrounding the workshop. In the quest to design an interesting program with relevant content and effective methods, details involving such mundane aspects as space, refreshments, parking, payments to guest speakers, name tags, audio-visual equipment, thank-you letters to people who helped, and so forth, often receive inadequate attention. Such inattention can lead to program failures: There is nothing that makes trainers look more silly, for instance, than fumbling with a videocassette recorder (VCR) that does not work. The "details" person would be in charge of making sure that mistakes like this do not occur. Wise training program directors make sure that the "details" person shares in any credit for successful programs. Such a person is important, and should be made to feel this way along with others who make more visible and possibly "glamorous" contributions, such as organizing a complex simulation about which participants were clearly enthusiastic. Reitz and Manning (1994) share a number of practical suggestions, such as attention to details, that are necessary for program success.

◆ The Need for Program Evaluation

Another person, not necessarily an employee of the organization offering training, is essential to the long-range success and improvement of programs. This person is the program evaluator who makes suggestions for how trainers can improve their work (formative evaluation) and who provides answers to the questions, "Has the training staff met its goals?" (summative evaluation). Too often, the potential contributions of evaluation specialists are downplayed as trainers try to wrap up one program so that they can begin marketing efforts to obtain other contracts. We believe that marketing efforts can be significantly improved if the contributions of evaluation specialists are carefully integrated into the long-term planning of organizations that offer training programs. Their contributions will be discussed in the next chapter.

6

The Evaluation
of Training Programs

◆ Reasons for Interest in Evaluation

Don Robbins was a professor in the Department of Management at a large state university. He taught courses in management development, human resources management in global perspective, and (through a cross-listed course in the Sociology Department) program evaluation. In addition to his teaching, research, and writing, he also carried out some consulting work with large firms in the city where he lived. He was also active in community activities, and many of these activities centered around his membership in the Rotary Club. Although enjoying the Rotarian lunches and club activities for their own sake, he also realized that other club members were prominent businesspeople who might have information about possible consulting jobs for him. One day, Don received a telephone call in his office. The conversation went like this:

> **Caller:** Don? Jack Pierce from the Rotary Club. I'm new in town, but we met at the last meeting. Do you remember my telling you that I'm with Barnsworth Manufacturing? We have a new training program here, and I hope you can help us out with it.

Don: What are the goals of the training program?

Jack: We are expanding into overseas markets in Germany, Indonesia, and Korea. The program is designed to help prepare managers, and their families, for the challenges they will face on overseas assignments.

Don: That sounds very forward looking. A lot of American companies don't pay much attention to intercultural training, thinking that doing business overseas is pretty much the same as doing it in the United States.

Jack: Well, I think so too. I was a participant in a Junior Year Abroad program in college, and I studied in France for a year. There was no special preparation for the students who participated, and let me tell you it was hard to adjust to the differences between studying in the United States and studying in France. So when I was in a position to introduce cross-cultural training at Barnsworth, I jumped at the chance.

Don: I cover cross-cultural training in my course on human resources management. How can I help you?

Jack: You can help me with evaluating the program. I don't know much about evaluation. The top brass here wants to know if the cross-cultural training program is any damn good and whether or not it's worth the cost.

Don: High-level executives often talk that way. They will also probably want to know whether or not people's performance, when stationed overseas, is better as a result of having been trained.

Jack: I have to write the executives a memo, within about 2 weeks, persuading them that the training program is worth continuing.

Don: I'll see if I can help with the contents of the memo you have to write. Can I ask you some basic questions now?

Jack: Sure, go ahead!

Don: Where are the people who will be trained?

Jack: We had the training program about 6 months ago, and the people are now in the three countries: Germany, Indonesia, and Korea.

Don: Was any information gathered from them before the training, and was this compared with information gathered after the training?

Jack: Not really. A lot of the program participants, though, told me that they liked the training and appreciated the opportunity to think about their upcoming overseas assignments.

Don: Was there a control or a comparison group, that is, were the people who received training compared with people who didn't receive training?

Jack: No, the company gave people time to participate, and all but two or three people who were to go overseas received training.

Don: Do you have figures on how much it costs to send someone overseas, and how much it costs to bring a family back to the United States if the assignment doesn't work out for some reason?

Jack: I've never seen figures like this. I suppose I could ask someone in the accounting office whether or not we could scrape something together.

Don: Do you have information on how many people, in past years, have not been successful on overseas assignments? For example, how many had to "be pulled out" before their assignments were completed?

Jack: Sorry, I've never seen information like that. It might not exist because Barnsworth hasn't been assigning people overseas for too many years.

Don: Can we get access to information about how the trained people are doing on their overseas assignments. For example, do we have access to ratings by supervisors in Germany, Indonesia, and Korea?

Jack: I don't think so. That information is considered pretty confidential at Barnsworth, and we'd have to get each trainee's permission to obtain access. Listen, Don, I know I haven't been able to answer "yes" very much, but I hope you can help out. I really want to see the training program continued, but I don't think it will be unless the memo I write on evaluation gets a good reception.

Don has probably participated in similar conversations with other people who are interested in starting or continuing intercultural training programs. People are rarely interested in evaluation until some outside force, usually a force with power, demands information on how good, how effective, and how helpful the program has been. When people receive demands for information on evaluation, they often turn to specialists and ask them for help. The requests for help, however, often seem to be appeals to magicians who can wave magic wands and produce proof about program quality and effectiveness. In the incident, is there anything that Don can do? The answer is, "No, not very much." One of the most important points about the development of good cross-cultural training programs is that evaluation specialists should be integrated into program planning from the very earliest stages. When integrated early, evaluation specialists can point to opportunities to gather information about (a) improving programs and (b) eventually developing persuasive arguments about their effectiveness.

◆ Conversations Between Intercultural Communication and Evaluation Specialists

When they participate in efforts to evaluate programs, intercultural communication specialists try to answer such questions as:

a. Can the training program be improved?
b. Have the goals of the training program been achieved?
c. Is the cross-cultural training program being evaluated of higher quality than other programs that could have been chosen for implementation?
d. Are there evaluation designs that allow information to be gathered on program effectiveness and that allow busy trainers to schedule their time efficiently?
e. Can the training program being evaluated provide guidance for setting up programs for other types of people? For example, can a program for businesspeople provide guidance for programs aimed at international students?
f. What are the beneficial effects of intercultural training as documented in good evaluation studies?

These are not easy questions to answer, and it takes a great deal of education and experience to deal with them effectively. Program evaluation is a specialized topic that is covered in a year-long series of graduate-level seminars at some universities. Excellent texts, literature reviews, and handbooks have been published (e.g., Berk & Rossi, 1990; Cook, Campbell, & Peracchio, 1991; Guttentag & Struening, 1975; Rossi & Freeman, 1989). The year-long seminars can involve upwards of 4,000 pages of reading as well as an internship in an organization where graduate students gain practical experience. Often, they evaluate a program within the organization as part of their internship. Given this amount of reading and needed experience, only limited goals can be achieved in this short treatment. The purposes of this chapter are to introduce some key ideas about program evaluation so that intercultural communication specialists can (a) have good discussions with and (b) integrate the talents of evaluation experts. Three topics will be discussed.

1. Some key concepts that are frequently used by evaluation specialists and those who would use their services, and the use of various research designs.
2. An introduction to various biases that can affect the results of evaluation studies.
3. The benefits of intercultural communication training as documented in various evaluation studies.

In the discussion of key points, research studies that have focused on the evaluation of actual intercultural communication training programs will be reviewed.

◆ Important Concepts for Discussions About Program Evaluation

When evaluation specialists sit down with administrators who are planning intercultural training programs, the following concepts will surely become central to their discussions.

FORMATIVE AND SUMMATIVE EVALUATION

Now a familiar distinction (Birnbrauer, 1987; Guttentag & Struening, 1975; Mathison, 1991), formative and summative evaluation refers to two different types of information that program planners can use. When efforts are focused on formative evaluation, information is gathered that will lead to program improvement. This improvement can occur within the time frame of one program (e.g., a "mid-course correction" taken at the end of the first day of a 2-day program), or the improvement can occur after a given program so that the next offering is more favorably received. The phrase "more favorably received" is carefully chosen because many formative evaluation methods focus on the responses of program participants. The most basic questions is, "Do they find the material presented useful and interesting or do they view the program as a waste of time?" There are few published studies that focus solely on formative evaluation of intercultural programs, and the reason reminds us that there are different goals that evaluation specialists strive to achieve. In formative evaluation, information is presented that assists efforts to improve programs within an organization. Such information focuses on what is perceived as important, what material should be dropped, what material should be added, what information is being learned, and so forth. Answers to these questions may be of very little interest to people in other organizations, and consequently the expense of publishing widely available journal articles based solely on formative evaluation is often a poor use of resources. Program participants often respond to questions about the following topics (Birnbrauer, 1987):

1. Has the program been well received? Specific questions ask program participants to give their opinions about how well planned the program seemed to be, how well prepared the trainers were, and whether or not there would be better uses of money than the amount spent on this program.

2. Are there corrections needed? Specific queries deal with the adequacy of the trainers, their abilities to answer questions that go beyond their prepared material, the desirability of more participant involvement (e.g., through active training methods such as role-playing), and the relative amount of time given to different topics.

3. Are the trainers' goals being met? Do program participants accept the importance of the topics covered, or is there

a great deal of resistance? Do participants seem engaged in the program, or are they bored? Are trainers able to cover the range of material that was planned, or do participants want to narrow the focus of the material covered?

In summative evaluation, information is gathered to answer the question, "Is the program effective." In everyday language, the question becomes, "Is the program any good?" Answers to these questions then lead to the very practical demand to present information that allows decision makers to either continue supporting a training program or dropping it because of its demonstrated ineffectiveness. Because effectiveness is conceptualized as helping people become more skillful communicators in interactions that transcend cultural barriers, the most impressive summative information is gathered after training ends. Good summative information can be gathered on how effective people are in communicating with culturally diverse individuals (as judged by those individuals), how long it takes them to perform effectively on their job in the other culture, how effective people are in solving problems, how they deal with the stress of intercultural living, whether or not they complete the full terms of their overseas assignments, and so forth.

Occasionally in all kinds of training programs, but perhaps more frequently for intercultural training (see Chapters 4 and 7), the results of formative and summative evaluations will be different. People may enjoy the training program (Trost, 1985) and report that it was worthwhile (formative), but they may not change anything about their work, their beliefs, their attitudes, or their behavior (issues addressed in a summative evaluation). Or, people may report that they disliked the training but later integrate much of what the trainers recommended into their actual behavior during their overseas assignments. Trifonovitch (1977) reported this pattern. As discussed in Chapter 5, Trifonovitch was in charge of programs that prepared people for assignments on remote Pacific islands. During training, they had to live in a manner similar to Pacific Islanders. Many American trainees did not like this one bit as they could not believe (during training) that they would have to gather their own food, make their own entertainment, and work without familiar technological aids. Consequently, they complained bitterly during training, "burning out" some of the staff (as discussed in Chapter 3). Years later, however, Trifonovitch received unsolicited letters from people, the same ones who complained bitterly, expressing how well prepared they were for their intercultural assignments. More information about summative evaluation will be presented in a later section of this chapter that deals with the measurement of program outcomes.

CONTROL AND COMPARISON GROUPS

Any discussion of summative evaluation leads to the analysis of control and comparison groups. The reason is that the most compelling evidence for the effectiveness of a program is often gathered by showing that people who have received training behave in a more effective manner than people who have not received the training. People who have not received training are referred to as members of the *control group* or the *comparison group*. The distinction between these two terms involves the amount of control the evaluator has in determining whether people receive training or not. The most straightforward and persuasive evaluation studies involve random assignment to either the training or no-training group (Campbell & Stanley, 1966). In random assignment, every person who might be a part of the evaluation study has an equal chance of being picked for the training group. Because the assumption behind randomization is that the resulting training and no-training groups are equivalent, the only differences people would eventually demonstrate on various measuring instruments must be due to training. When the evaluator can employ randomization in the selection of training program participants, the people who do not receive training are known as members of the control group. When evaluators do not have control over the decision whether people receive training or not, they often search for a similar group of people who have not received training. This group of people who bear similarity to the training group, but who were not randomly assigned to a no-training group, should be called a comparison group.

As an example of the search for a comparison group, Befus (1988) offered intercultural training to 64 North Americans who were studying Spanish at the *Instituto de Lingua Española* in San José, Costa Rica. For a number of reasons, it was difficult if not impossible to randomly assign 32 of the students to a training group and 32 to a control group. One reason was that the 64 students interacted with each other frequently, and any helpful information that might have been presented to the training group participants would have been shared with friends in the control group. Given that she could not form a control group, Befus searched for the possibility of a comparison group. She developed one by working with North Americans who had been students at the *Institute de Lingua Española* during the previous school term. These students had presumably been faced with cultural differences in Costa Rica that demanded adjustment and that perhaps caused culture-shock reactions, but they had not participated in a training program. Befus compared reports of stress (see Chapter 3) among members of the training group with the reports among members of this comparison group. Given that members of the training group reported less stress subsequent to the program, Befus argued that her program was effective.

USING CONTROL GROUPS WHEN POSSIBLE

While the formation of comparison groups can seem at first glance to be reasonable, and while at times they are essential to carrying out the best evaluation efforts possible, there are difficulties that they bring. The major difficulty is that people in a comparison group may be different to start with, and consequently positive effects that might be attributed to training may be due to qualities of the people in the training group. This problem can exist even when efforts are made to make the training and comparison groups as similar as possible. For example, Befus (1988) took steps to ensure that her groups were similar. People in the two groups were similar in terms of the number of males and females, "marital status, amount of previous cross-cultural exposure, level of education, age, religious affiliation, previous language experience, and amount of exposure to subcultures within North America" (p. 391). Although this is an impressive list, differences in stress levels could be due to other factors not addressed by Befus. For example, people in the comparison group could have been different in terms of aspects of their personalities, such as general anxiety level. This general anxiety level may have led to more self-reported stress among comparison group members than among training group members. This type of analysis admittedly sounds like carping and nit-picking, but such factors must be taken into account during serious evaluation efforts. Especially when there is competition for funds to support various programs (e.g., more Spanish language study compared to support of the cross-cultural training program), administrators must present solid evaluative evidence to bolster their recommendations for how funds should be used.

Why aren't control groups employed more frequently than they are? One reason is that many program administrators feel that there are ethical problems with denying training to people who want it. An ideal study, from the viewpoint of sophisticated summative evaluation, would begin by identifying people who want training. Assume that 60 people sign up. Then the people would be randomly assigned to a training and to a control group, perhaps by putting all names in a box, mixing them up, and drawing them out. Thirty people would be assigned to the training group and 30 to the control group. After the program and after people have actually assumed their intercultural assignments, summative information would be gathered. The evaluator would determine whether or not the program led to benefits for the training group compared to the control group. For instance, symptoms of stress could be measured, and information on job productivity could be gathered.

The ethical dilemma for program administrators and evaluation specialists is that they are denying the benefits of training to some people. The basic conclusion that good training has positive benefits is well established (Black & Medenthall, 1990; Brislin, Landis, & Brandt, 1983; Cushner, 1989). Some of these benefits will be reviewed later in this chapter as part of the discussion of outcome measures in evaluation. The fact that good training leads to benefits, of course, does not mean that any one training program being currently evaluated will result in benefits. It does mean, however, that the possibility of benefits exists and that people without training may experience cross-cultural difficulties for which they could have been better prepared. Professionals involved in cross-cultural training face an ethical dilemma. They know that the use of control groups provides the most persuasive information about training's effects, but people in the control group may experience problems that could have been prevented. Are there ways of resolving this dilemma?

THE WAIT-CONTROL DESIGN

One evaluation design, when successfully employed, involves a compromise between the need to gather good information on program effectiveness and the need to give training to all who want it. At times, it even works into the busy schedules of program administrators and allows them to schedule their time most productively. The design is called "wait-control," and variants of it have been used in a number of research studies (e.g., Ganster, Mayes, Sime, & Tharp, 1982; Ilola, 1989). Its features are clearest when used in an example. Assume that 60 people in an organization want to participate in an intercultural communication training program. The randomization process takes place, and 30 are assigned to a "training: time 1" group, and 30 are assigned to a "training: time 2" group. This second group is also called the "wait-control." In a pictorial form, the design can be depicted as follows (see Table 6.1). Using the shorthand developed by Campbell and Stanley (1966), "X" refers to the

TABLE 6.1
The Wait-Control Design

Randomization	Observations: 1	Time 1	Observations: 2	Time 2	Observations: 3
Group 1	O	X	O		O
Group 2	O		O	X	O

training program and "O" refers to observations or measurements of program effects. In our example, let's assume that the "Xs" are the responsibility of the program administrator, that the "Os" are the responsibility of the evaluation specialist, and that Time 1 and Time 2 refer to a 2-week training program.

Information is gathered from all people at the point called "Observations: 1." For example, their ability to solve the sorts of critical incidents presented throughout this book could be assessed [an approach taken by Cushner (1989) and Ilola (1989)]. Then people in Group 1 receive the 2-week training program, while the people in Group 2 wait for training. At the point called "Observations: 2," information is again gathered from all 60 people. At this point, there is a true training group and a true control group: If the training is effective, people in that group should score higher on various measuring instruments. For example, people in the trained group should be able to solve more critical incidents (that they haven't seen before) than people in the wait-control group (Cushner, 1989; Ilola, 1989). Then people in Group 2 receive the 2-week training program while people in Group 1 go back to their jobs within their organization. At the point called "Observations: 3," measures are again gathered from all people. People in the second group should demonstrate increases compared to their performance at observation points 1 and 2. In addition, people in the first training group should demonstrate that they have maintained the benefits of training as measured earlier at observation point 2.

From the organization's standpoint, the major advantage to this design is that all people desirous of training participate in a program. From the evaluator's standpoint, the advantage is that information is available about program benefits because there is a point (Observations: 2) at which there is a true training and a true control group. Further, information is available (Observations: 3) on the retention of program benefits. For many intercultural communication training programs, however, this is not a perfect design. If evaluators want to measure long-term benefits, such as job performance after overseas assignment and amount of stress experienced a year after training, the use of a wait-control can be less than ideal. If the program lasts 2 weeks, as in our example, then long-term benefits can be assessed only after all participants have received training. Long-term benefits would be assessed at a point that would be marked "Observations: 4" in the diagram, and such benefits would be assessed long after measurements gathered at the earlier "Observations: 3" point. Note that by this later time, all people have received training and there is no longer a control group.

The wait-control design is very useful and brings up issues that program planners and evaluators should discuss. The design is most applicable when measures of effectiveness can be gathered shortly after training and when there is still a control group (Observations: 2 in the diagram). Examples of such measures (more will be reviewed later in the chapter) include facts learned about life in other cultures, ability to analyze critical incidents involving intercultural contact in one's own life, performance on measuring instruments designed to assess intercultural sensitivity, and rated performance in actual encounters or role-playing involving interactions between program participants and people from very different cultural backgrounds (see review of study by Collett, 1971, in Chapter 4).

CONTROL GROUPS WHOSE MEMBERS
RECEIVE OTHER TRAINING

Are there other designs that maintain a control group, allow for the assessment of long-term impacts, and fulfill ethical obligations to offer training to all who desire it? This is a large

TABLE 6.2
Comparison Between Programs

Randomization	Observations: 1	Time 1	Observations: 2	Observations: 3
Group 1	O	X	O	long-term follow-up
Group 2	O	other training	O	long-term follow-up

set of requirements to fulfill, but the answer is "yes." However, there is a set of conditions that places limits on the number of research studies that allow a "yes" answer.

The research design to be discussed here calls for a training group that receives a newly developed program that the evaluator wants to assess and a control group whose members receive another type of training program. This other training program should be well established and have a reputation for effectiveness since it would be unethical to assign people randomly to a poorly conceived program. This concept of a comparison between a newly developed program and an established program is similar to comparisons in the development of new drugs. When pharmaceutical companies propose a new drug, it is not enough to demonstrate that it is effective against a disease. Federal regulations require that the new drug is demonstrably more beneficial (or as beneficial with fewer side effects) than other drugs already on the market. The diagram for this design is shown in Table 6.2.

People who want training are randomly assigned to one of two groups. Given that the assignment is random, the use of the term *control group* is appropriate. Measures are taken, and then all people receive training. "X" in the diagram refers to the newly developed program and "other training" refers to another program, perhaps one that the organization has been using for a number of years. Observations are taken shortly after training and a significant amount of time after training. In cross-cultural studies, the long-term follow-up is sometimes carried out after people have assumed their overseas assignments or assignments within their own countries that demand extensive intercultural interactions. The evaluator looks for evidence, at Observations 2 and 3, that people in the newly developed training program demonstrate more intercultural effectiveness than people in the control group.

The use of this design becomes clearer if an actual study is reviewed. Cushner (1989) worked with 50 international exchange students in New Zealand who were sponsored by AFS International, one of the most active organizations dedicated to sponsoring intercultural experiences for adolescents. The 50 exchange students, all of whom were to attend high school in New Zealand, came from 14 different countries. Cushner was interested in evaluating a new training program based on the culture general assimilator (Brislin et al., 1986), a set of intercultural materials that was discussed in Chapter 2. By a flip of the coin, 28 of the students were randomly assigned to receive training based on the culture general assimilator. Twenty-two of the students were assigned to another training program that had been long used by AFS International in New Zealand, and that consisted of "small group activities and discussions around such issues as self-identity, hopes and fears, local home and family life, and adjustment" (Cushner, 1989, p. 132). These 22 students used materials developed and distributed by AFS International, and consequently is called the "AFS materials" group in this discussion. Both training programs consisted of four sessions lasting 1½ hours each, and that took place over a 2-day period. This period corresponded to the 2 days between their arrival in New Zealand and the day they left the training site to join host families in various New Zealand towns and cities. All trainees completed the measuring instruments immediately after training, and they provided other information related to their intercultural adjustment 3 and 6 months into their homestay experiences.

Cushner found that students in the culture assimilator training group showed a number of benefits compared to those in the AFS materials group. Members of the culture assimilator group were able to solve more difficult critical incidents and were better able to analyze problematic intercultural incidents (in which they were participants) in their own lives. Three months after training, members of the culture assimilator group expressed feelings that they had more control over problems that might face them during their everyday lives in New Zealand. Feelings that one lacks control over everyday problems is a symptom of culture shock. Six months after training, these same students were better able to suggest ways of solving problems (known as the *means* of problem solving; Spivak, Platt, & Shire, 1976) that faced them. In addition, another long-term effect (although not statistically significant) was that there were fewer major problems in the culture assimilator group during their stay in New Zealand. "Major problems" is a carefully chosen term, because it refers to problems so severe that adolescents (a) had to leave one host family and find another or (b) leave New Zealand prematurely and return to their own countries.

Why isn't this the perfect design? One reason is that program administrators and evaluators are almost working against themselves when they use this design. When the alternative training program is reasonable and when trainers have experience using it (both true of the AFS materials), then it is very hard to develop a new program that is more effective. In addition, when both programs are equally effective as shown by the evaluation data, there is no assurance that training of any kind is more effective than no training. Consider Table 6.2 again: If both programs are equally effective, there is no control group that allows statements to be made about whether trained people have gained benefits that control group participants have not.

There is one other type of study where this design (sometimes called "control group also receives training") is appropriate. In some organizations, the concept that people must receive cross-cultural training is well established. When this is true, then program administrators and evaluators can concentrate on developing training modules, or sets of materials, that are useful for very different purposes. One module might deal with gender differences, another with working well across cultural boundaries, another on understanding nonverbal behaviors, another on working through language interpreters, and so forth (Brislin & Yoshida, 1994). When these modules are used, evaluators can predict very specific benefits and then assess people to determine whether the benefits exist or not. For example, if a gender differences module is used, evaluators can predict that female co-workers will report, months after training, that people who worked with this module show respect for women and their contributions. Various modules can be compared with one another using the "control group also receives training" design. The purpose is not to test the general question of whether training is effective or not, but rather to test the more specific questions of whether specific modules lead to specific benefits. Such information is very helpful for the development of intercultural communication training programs because various administrators can formulate program goals and then select from among a number of approaches, methods, and modules whose effectiveness has been established.

◆ Avoiding Biases in Evaluation Studies

In addition to providing persuasive information about the benefits of a training program, careful evaluation designs allow arguments to be made that the measured benefits are not due to other factors. The term *biases* is used frequently to refer to other factors, such as preexisting traits of the program participants or the pleasant personalities of the training personnel (in contrast to the training itself). More specifically (Campbell & Stanley, 1966), biases refer to factors that threaten the conclusion that a training program has led to various benefits. Six of the biases discussed most frequently among program administrators and evaluators (more are discussed in Campbell & Stanley,

1966; Cook et al., 1991; Rossi & Freeman, 1989) will be examined here.

THE SELECTION BIAS

When the effects of training may be due to features of the program participants rather than to the program content, then the selection bias must be discussed. The possibility of a selection bias is especially threatening when the evaluation design does not have a control group. When the study by Befus (1988) was discussed earlier in this chapter, the possibility that people in her comparison group had higher levels of anxiety was mentioned. If certain people who are selected for either the training or comparison groups possess qualities that may affect the results of the evaluation study, then confidence in the results has to weaken. The best way to overcome a selection bias is to assign people randomly to the training or the control group. In this way, any preexisting qualities of people (such as anxiety level) are equalized prior to the start of training.

Another aspect of evaluation that invites discussions of a selection bias stems from the use of questionnaires (Cogswell & Stubblefield, 1988; Dixon, 1987; Trost, 1985). Many evaluation specialists fear that an overreliance on questionnaires leads to a bias given the reluctance of many trainees to give their honest reactions. So as not to offend members of the training staff, many trainees may simply report that they enjoyed training even if they had reservations. This reaction is especially possible if the training staff consists of very pleasant, congenial people who are clearly trying to make a living offering programs to various companies. Rather than interfere with the trainers' livelihood, program participants make a point of saying nice things. To avoid this bias, evaluators make other types of measurements, such as ratings of respect shown when trainees interact with people from other cultures, observations of on-the-job performance, the ability to solve difficult critical incidents, the ability to suggest exact ways of solving problems, and so forth.

THE HISTORY BIAS

When experiences in people's lives can affect the results of training, then the history bias must be discussed. The term refers either to events in people's personal histories, such as previous intercultural experience, or events that occur at the same time as training. For example, consider a training program that is organized to prepare executives for sojourns in Germany. If the program was held during the week that the Berlin Wall was torn down, then evaluators would have to worry whether the results gathered after training were due to program content or to this major symbolic event. The history bias can be problematic in the wait-control design if there is a long period of time between assignment to the control group and the start of training (at Time 2, as previously depicted in Table 6.1). If the time period is long, events may happen that can be as impactful as training. Consider international students who have recently arrived in the United States. If they are asked to wait 3 days for their training, they may happen to meet some American students who are attending the same school. If those American students act in a friendly manner, tell the sojourners about key points such as how to register for the best courses, and take them on tours around the campus and nearby town, these events can easily be as impactful as a good training program.

THE MORTALITY BIAS

Especially when an evaluation study takes place over a long period of time, participants may either drop out or become unavailable due to various changes in their lives. *Mortality* refers to the loss of people in either the training group(s), control group, or comparison group. For example, Befus (1988) offered intercultural training to 64 North Americans who were studying in Costa Rica. Fifty-two people accepted her invitation and signed up for training, and in our experience this is a good response because the training was voluntary and the participants' free time was involved. However, 20 participants dropped out over the course of the 6-week program and consequently only 32 were available for final observations that were essential for a verdict concerning program effectiveness. Evaluators have to wonder about the representativeness of the final 32 people. Were they typical of the original 52 that signed up for the program? Perhaps the final 32 were the people most interested in intercultural interaction and most concerned about understanding culture and cultural differences. This initial level of interest could influence observations made at the conclusion of training.

BIASES DUE TO REACTIVE EFFECTS

At times, people who find themselves selected for training may view themselves as privileged and as singled out for special attention. Further, especially if the training appears well-thought-out and potentially beneficial, participants may develop favorable views of their organization for choosing them. These possibilities are reactions to *participation in training,* not to the content of the training. These reactions are sometimes called "Hawthorne effects" because they were documented in a classic study that took place at the Hawthorne plant of the Western Electric Company in Cicero, IL (see Landy, 1989, for a discussion). One of the surprising findings of that research was that many kinds of changes in the organization led to greater worker productivity. One of the few common elements underlying the changes was that workers felt special given the attention they received from management and prestigious scholars.

When evaluators talk about "controlling for Hawthorne effects," they are referring to biases brought on by the special attention that accompanies training. Cushner (1989) thought carefully about this possibility, and his analysis was one reason for the choice of a design in which all participants received training (as reviewed previously). He reported, "There is no reason to believe that any [participant] would perceive oneself as receiving anything special during the weekend as all subjects

received the same number of hours of good training by concerned and experienced representatives from local AFS chapters" (p. 132).

COMPENSATORY TREATMENT OF THE CONTROL GROUP

The ethical qualms that administrators experience when
designating a training group and a no-training control group
have been referred to several times. Administrators do not like to
deny training to people who desire it. Assume that the training
program is to last 4 weeks, and that participants are to be taken
off their jobs for 2 hours a day to attend training sessions. If
they add the "compensatory treatment of the control group bias,"
the administrators may unconsciously treat control group members in special ways to make up for the decision that delegat-
ed these people to the no-training group. They may approve
requests for leave, overtime with double pay, and attendance at lectures in the community that bear a relationship to the organization's international goals. The treatment the control group
members receive may lead to benefits that are similar to those
demonstrated by members of the training group. Even if the
training was beneficial, it would be difficult to document this
fact given the compensatory treatment received by control group
members.

COMPENSATORY ACTIVITIES
AMONG CONTROL GROUP MEMBERS

At times, control group members learn that there is a training
group and become resentful. As a result, they organize and engage
in activities that develop group cohesiveness and morale. They
may talk among themselves and say, "I don't know why those
other people got to be in the training group and we didn't. But
we're just as good as those other people. Let's do important
things around here and show management that we're right!"

The alternative name for this bias is the "John Henry" effect,
and this is our favorite name for a term used by evaluators given

our interest in music. John Henry was a steel driver who could hold a heavy hammer in each hand and drive steel into rocks to cut tunnels for railroads. One day, an inventor with a steam drill came to the work sight and argued that he could cut a longer tunnel than any worker. So John Henry competed against the steam drill, perhaps resentful of the positive attention that management lavished on the inventor. John Henry won the contest because he drove a 14-foot tunnel while the steam drill had to stop at 9 feet. The tragedy of the story is that John Henry broke a blood vessel during the contest and died. In one of American folk music's best known tributes to feminism, his wife Polly took over his railroad job to earn money for the support of their children.

Whenever they discuss the best ways to document the benefits of training programs, administrators and evaluators should examine the various biases that can threaten the conclusion of "positive effects." This list of six discussed here is a good start, and others can be found in the scholarly literature on program evaluation (e.g., Campbell & Stanley, 1966; Cook et al., 1991; Rossi & Freeman, 1989). The purpose of this exercise is to rule out explanations that could be due to biases, and to build a strong set of arguments that the program leads to genuine benefits. Researchers interested in intercultural training have involved themselves as evaluators of many different types of programs, and they have documented a wide variety of benefits. Knowledge of these benefits is very useful to program administrators and evaluators.

◆ The Benefits of Intercultural Training

Over the past 25 years, a large number of researchers have become involved in the careful evaluation of various intercultural training programs. The many benefits they have documented can provide very helpful guidance to administrators contemplating the development of new programs. Administrators can realistically adopt the goals of training represented in this list because they have been achieved by others. Evaluation specialists can benefit because the studies listed give information on important topics such as study design, measuring instruments, and the development of theory. In all these studies, people receiving training were compared with either a control group or a comparison group. When there were potential biases, as in the study by Befus (1988; as discussed above, especially the mortality bias), researchers presented a reasonable set of arguments that the potential threats to validity did not overwhelm the conclusion of positive benefits. The benefits can be organized in a manner similar to the coverage of training content in this book: effects on people's thinking, on their attitudes and emotions, and on their behavior.

POSITIVE EFFECTS INVOLVING PEOPLE'S THINKING AND KNOWLEDGE DEVELOPMENT

The benefits due to knowledge development are probably the easiest to measure because people can demonstrate changes in thinking and knowledge acquisition on paper-and-pencil tests and questionnaires.

1. Greater understanding of host nationals from the host nationals' own point of view (Albert & Adamapoulous, 1980; Landis, Brislin, & Hulgus, 1985; Landis, Brislin, Swanner, Tzeng, & Thomas, 1985). One way of measuring this potential benefit is to develop a test of knowledge that people in the host culture commonly hold. Then, after training, people about to live in that culture are tested for their acquisition of this knowledge. For example, members of a certain culture may express widespread agreement with the statement, "In our culture, a response of 'I'll think about it' is more likely to mean 'no' than 'yes.' " After training, evaluators can present such statements to program participants to determine if they have learned the host viewpoint regarding this piece of knowledge.

2. A decrease in the use of negative stereotypes in thinking about hosts (Albert & Adamapoulous, 1980; Landis & Tzeng,

1981). At times, program participants become very sophisticated in their ability to recognize stereotypical conclusions about other groups. If the measuring instrument allows free responses, they write reactions such as "I can't respond to an oversimplification like this," or "I need far more context before I can answer."

3. The development of complex rather than oversimplified thinking about another culture (Gim, Atkinson, & Kim, 1991; Landis, Day, McGrew, Miller, & Thomas, 1976; Malpass & Salancik, 1977; Wade & Bernstein, 1991). There are two uses of the term *complexity* under discussion here. One is that many factors, rather than only one or two, are given consideration when making decisions. For example, working with international students, advisers would be guilty of oversimplified thinking if they considered only the students' progress toward their degrees. More complex thinking would take into account the students' finances, the needs of their families, the work they will do when they return to their home countries, the variety of reasons they have for pursuing their studies in another country, and so forth. The other use of the term refers to the recognition of various viewpoints as held by people in different cultures. Recall the incident that introduced Chapter 1. Shirley was demonstrating complex thinking when she was able to recognize how Fakir approached the task of proposing a thesis topic and how American professors typically approach the same task.

4. In longer programs (approximately 10 weeks), increases in the general attitude called "world-mindedness" as well as greater knowledge about one's own culture (Steinkalk & Taft, 1979). World-mindedness refers to an interest and concern about events in various countries, not just one's own country and the countries in which one has lived. People often are stimulated to think carefully about their own culture, sometimes for the first time, given the differences they learn about during training. By analyzing reasons for the differences, they are forced to think about the reasons why people in their own culture behave the way they do.

5. The ability to solve difficult critical incidents that demand a knowledge of culture and cultural differences, and the ability to analyze critical incidents in one's own life (Cushner, 1989; Ilola, 1989). As people learn how to keep increasing their knowledge and sophistication, they develop the ability to suggest solutions to critical incidents that demand more knowledge than was covered during the formal training program.

POSITIVE EFFECTS INVOLVING PEOPLE'S AFFECTIVE REACTIONS

Affective reactions include people's attitudes, self-concepts, emotions, and feelings of comfort in another culture rather then stressful reactions. Although most studies to date are based on people's self-reports, we predict that future research will see the addition of more objective indicators such as measures of blood pressure (Charlesworth, Williams, & Baer, 1984) reports by others who know program participants well, careful records of visits to physicians, and so forth.

6. Increases in feelings of self-confidence that allow people to meet the challenges brought on by intercultural contact (O'Brien & Plooij, 1976; Worchel & Mitchell, 1972). If people are confident about their abilities to deal with cultural differences, they can continue to seek out opportunities to learn more long after the formal training program ends.

7. Greater enjoyment among people as they interact with hosts (Landis, Brislin, & Hulgus, 1985; Randolph, Landis, & Tzeng, 1977). Especially strong tests of this effect would involve questions about people's free time. When intercultural contact is not demanded (e.g., receptions for visiting dignitaries at work), do people interact with hosts during those times when they have a wide range of choices about their activities?

8. Increases in feelings, from people's own perspectives, that they have good working relations with hosts (Earley, 1987; Landis et al., 1985) and that they are enjoying their overseas assignments (Gudykunst, Hammer, & Wiseman, 1977). Of course,

this one measure is not enough to claim success for a program. These feelings of positive working relationships must be reciprocated by hosts (as discussed below).

9. Decreases in reported levels of stress (Befus, 1988; Johnson, 1989). For example (compared to others in control or comparison groups), people report fewer headaches, fewer difficulties trying to sleep, fewer episodes involving stomach upset, and so forth.

POSITIVE EFFECTS INVOLVING PEOPLE'S BEHAVIOR

Program administrators and evaluators are correct when they argue that changes in people's knowledge and feelings are extremely important. However, evidence about changes in people's visible behaviors will always be more persuasive to outsiders who make decisions concerning the amount of support that training will receive.

10. Better interpersonal relations in work groups composed of people from different cultural backgrounds (Earley, 1987; Fiedler, Mitchell, & Triandis, 1971). This can be an extremely important benefit in cultures where there is the strong expectation that people will work smoothly together, will share knowledge effectively, and will place a high value on harmonious relations.

11. Greater ease when interacting with hosts, as perceived by the hosts themselves (Landis, Brislin, & Hulgus, 1985; Randolph, Landis, & Tzeng, 1977; Weldon, Carlston, Rissman, Slobodin, & Triandis, 1975). Measures of this potential benefit are gathered from hosts rather than from program participants. One way of measuring training's effects is to have people from other cultures interact with graduates of training programs and controls. After the interactions, they can rate participants and controls (without knowing who received training and who did not) on indicators such as amount of cultural knowledge demonstrated, respect shown, ease and comfort during the interaction,

and so forth (Collett, 1971; Landis, Brislin, & Hulgus, 1985; Weldon et al., 1975).

12. More sophistication when setting and working toward goals in other cultures (Katz, 1977) and increases in the ability to formulate solutions to problems (Cushner, 1989). A greater sophistication often involves a move toward reality. Many program participants begin training with romantic, overly optimistic views: They will make many friends quickly in the other culture, they will experience no culture shock, and they will have access to key information just as they do in their own country. Good training can guide people toward a more realistic outlook and can encourage people to develop skills useful in reacting to the problems that they will inevitably encounter.

13. Better job performance (Earley, 1987; Johnson, 1989; O'Brien, Fiedler, & Hewett, 1970; Westwood & Barker, 1990). As we discussed in Chapter 4, good training should be based on behaviors that are identifiable as helpful in people's work in other cultures. Then, these behaviors can be practiced. For example, in the study by O'Brien and his colleagues (1970), medical volunteers went to Honduras to inoculate hosts against diseases. Volunteers who participated in intercultural training gave more inoculations, and one interpretation of this finding is that they learned behaviors that allowed them to gain the trust and confidence of hosts. In the Westwood and Barker (1990) study, international students who went through a complex training program received better grades and dropped out of college less frequently. One interpretation is that specific behaviors could be identified for training: study habits, asking hosts for advice about term paper selection, developing a support group, and so forth. In the Johnson (1989) study, Mexican-American children whose families went through training were less disruptive in classrooms within Houston, Texas, school districts. Here, training can address problems that cause disruptions and can also cover definitions of "disruptive behavior" that can be culturally different (see treatment of categorization and differentiation, Chapter 2).

As discussed in Chapter 4, our strong recommendation is that training give more attention to identifiable behaviors. In addition to excellent program content, a focus on behaviors makes evaluation studies more impactful when evidence can be presented that people have changed their behavior (e.g., visible job performance) in desirable directions.

◆ Evaluation: Its Role in Continuing the Support of Intercultural Training

In addition to providing important information central to the improvement of programs, evaluators can make other contributions. One, as seen in the critical incident that introduced this chapter, is that they assist program administrators defend the continued funding of intercultural training programs. In almost all the organizations that we know, the budget for training programs is not large and there is a great deal of competition for available funds. If program administrators cannot convince executives that intercultural training is effective, then the funds will go to other types of training. We recommended attention to measures of actual behavior, not only because they provide important information that can be integrated into books like this one, but also because behavioral measures provide the most convincing evidence of program effectiveness. When a concept such as "convincing funders" is treated, we are moving away from discussions of intercultural training itself and are beginning to examine the larger social context in which training exists. Intercultural training does not exist in a vacuum: It takes place in societies where many administrators are competing for program funds, where young professionals want to make a living by offering training, and where many potential clients do not know how to deal with the issues stemming from the increased intercultural interactions they are experiencing. In the final chapter, we discuss some of these issues that will affect the future of intercultural communication training.

7

Issues Affecting the Future of Intercultural Training

◆ A Phone Call to an Experienced Trainer

Mary Carlson is the founder and president of a small consulting firm that, as one of its offerings, organizes intercultural training programs. The firm is located in a medium-sized city in the United States. Mary also teaches, in her role as an affiliate faculty member, a course in intercultural communication at a nearby university. She has a good reputation in her field and is also known as being very accessible to newcomers who want to investigate job possibilities in training. One day, she received a telephone call from a graduating senior at the university.

Caller: Is this Mary Carlson? You haven't met me, but my name is Henry Foster. I'm a student at the university and I graduate in a few months. I majored in psychology but I got your name from the communication department.

Mary: I teach a course for the communication department. What can I do for you?

Henry: I'll be looking for a job when I graduate. I hear there are opportunities for people who can offer training programs to organizations that have various international concerns.

172

Mary: There are some opportunities, although I have to say right away that there are more people who want jobs in training than the number of openings.

Henry: For the last 2 years, one of my apartment mates has been a student from Germany. He went through a program to prepare him for his studies in the United States. It was called a cross-cultural training program. It sounded very interesting. I'd like to explore the possibility of a career in which I could organize this sort of program.

Mary: There are a few such jobs. Have you had any coursework? I don't think you took my course in intercultural communication, although there is another professor who offers it.

Henry: No, I can't think of much relevant coursework. I really became interested just by living with my apartment mate from Germany.

Mary: One of my pieces of advice is that people examine their skills to identify those that are relevant to careers in training. More than extensive intercultural experience is necessary. For example, people offering training programs must be very good public speakers, and they must be able to market their programs to paying customers. Have you had courses in these areas?

Henry: I had one course in public speaking. I never had a course in marketing. Actually, I wouldn't be very interested in that aspect. I would want to actually organize and offer the training programs.

Mary: There are many opportunities to give training programs, but not all organizations can pay a decent fee. Many people ask me to give programs, such as schoolteachers and social workers, but these people don't usually have much money. To earn a decent salary, a person has to sell programs to people who can pay: businesses, government agencies, colleges, and so forth. I look at the fee that the university pays me, for instance, as part of the yearly salary that I pay myself. I went to the communication department and offered to teach. The chairperson didn't come to me.

Henry: I was never very good at selling anything to others. Are there other activities associated with training that I could learn about? I'll do anything to help if you let me spend time in your organization—typing, photocopying, library work, and so forth?

Mary: I'm giving a workshop this coming Friday at 4:00 P.M. Why don't you come? I'll ask you to do a few things to help out, but mostly you could observe how a training program is put together.

Henry: O.K. I'll see you at your office a little before 4:00 P.M. on Friday.

That Friday, Henry showed up at 4:10 P.M. because he underestimated the amount of time it would take to get to Mary's office. Upon his arrival, he found that the program participants were delayed and that they agreed to make up the lost time the next day (a Saturday). While waiting for the participants, Mary asked Henry to photocopy some handouts for the revised material that she would be covering tomorrow. Henry started to complain.

Henry: You mean we have to work on Saturday? I've always kept weekends free so that I could spend time with my friends.

Mary: Trainers often have to work on weekends and also during evening hours. Especially with paying clients, we have to work when they want programs to be offered. These clients sometimes want workshops offered outside of normal working hours. Have you photocopied the handouts yet?

Henry: I was hoping that I would be doing something more important than photocopying. I think I have a very unique perspective on intercultural communication. I was hoping that I would be given some time with the trainees.

This conversation, which is a composite of many that we and our colleagues have had with potential newcomers, raises a number of issues that are important for the future of intercultural communication training. In its most general form, the question addressed in this chapter is: "How can we prepare ourselves so that there is a good future for intercultural training?" To address this important topic, four more specific issues are addressed:

1. What should young professionals do if they want to prepare themselves for careers that will include the organization and delivery of intercultural communication training programs?

2. What are some advantages of, and concerns about, the development of university-level coursework in applied intercultural communication?

3. Will the careers of these young people be more successful if they become more sophisticated about power, about competition for resources within organizations, and about relations between themselves and powerful decision makers?

4. Any professional specialization can be enhanced if its proponents take a long-range view of its development. What are some aspects of intercultural communication training that will benefit from long-range planning?

As with the sections in Chapter 5 dealing with tacit knowledge held by experienced trainers, the material on career development among newcomers and ethical concerns benefited from the work of Ptak et al. (1994).

◆ Newcomers Who Want to Become Involved in Intercultural Training

Many people who become exposed to the field of intercultural communication training become extremely fascinated and begin to explore the possibility of earning a living by offering training programs. Almost always, they become interested because of an intense intercultural experience in their own lives: a year spent studying in another culture, a long vacation in another country, a romance with a person from another culture, a 2-year period with the Peace Corps or other international organization, volunteer work among members of culturally diverse groups within their own country, and so forth. Many times, people want to explore job possibilities without knowledge and experience that goes beyond their own intercultural encounters. As has become clear from the material covered in the previous chapters, personal experiences are not enough. In addition, potential intercultural trainers have to have extensive knowledge (Chapter 2), experience with handling a wide variety of emotional reactions (Chapter 3), the ability to identify different behaviors considered appropriate in various cultures (Chapter 4), expertise in organizing the flow of material and experiences in training programs (Chapter 5), a basic understanding of program evaluation (Chapter 6), and so forth. Where can this range of information and experiences be found?

In addition to extensive reading (e.g., the materials in this volume's Reference section), there are three basic answers. People can begin to go beyond their own intercultural experiences and learn about the much broader issues in training by: (a) choosing courses in college wisely, (b) becoming an apprentice to experienced intercultural trainers, and (c) participating in workshops organized by various organizations devoted to the advancement of intercultural communication training. The first two approaches will be discussed here, and the names of organizations that offer various workshops will be indicated throughout this chapter.

RELEVANT COLLEGE COURSES

In a survey of members of the Society for Intercultural Education, Training, and Research, Harman and Briggs (1991) asked members about the most appropriate college departments where relevant coursework could be found. Members answered that courses in anthropology, sociology, linguistics, psychology, and speech/communication were most useful. Courses in these areas will acquaint people with basic knowledge upon which they can draw when organizing training programs, especially the knowledge component (Chapter 2). More specifically, courses in cultural anthropology, small groups (offered in various colleges by sociology, communication, and psychology departments), language and culture, a foreign language (4 years), social structure, cross-cultural psychology, social psychology, counseling psychology, intercultural communication, and communication theory are especially useful. Some colleges offer a course that covers many of the topics in this book: The course is variously called intercultural communication training, applied intercultural communication, or applied cross-cultural psychology. To this list of courses stimulated by the analysis of Harman and Briggs (1991), we also suggest examining the offerings of business schools to determine if courses in human resources management and international management are offered.

In a study of the tacit knowledge held by experienced trainers, Ptak et al. (1994) asked respondents to talk about information that they know now and that they *wished they knew* when starting out in their profession. Several indicated additional courses that they wished they had taken. Several mentioned that they wished they had more exposure to the world of business through courses in accounting, finance, and economics. One of intercultural training's basic facts is that to earn a living, people must offer training to those willing and able to pay. The largest number of "paying customers" will be found in business and industry. If people have taken a number of basic business courses, they will be able to talk intelligently with businesspeople, recognize their concerns, and be able to tailor training to these concerns. Several other respondents also looked to business schools and recommended courses in marketing and sales. These respondents argued that many newcomers to intercultural training feel that they can wait by their phone and field a wide variety of requests from large numbers of organizations. In reality, trainers have to be very assertive in selling and marketing their offerings. Especially in large cities, there is a great deal of competition among trainers for the attention of organizations whose administrators are willing to offer reasonable fees for intercultural programs.

Other experienced trainers recommended that people take as many courses in public speaking as possible. These trainers recognized that public speaking skills are essential both to acquiring contracts and to offering good programs. They recommended that people go beyond the one required course in public speaking that some schools demand. Instead, they recommended that people take advanced courses on such topics as persuasive speaking, extemporaneous speaking, rhetoric, acting, and debate. Courses in debate are especially important for the development of skills that allow trainers to answer difficult questions and to deal with trainees who disagree strongly about program goals and choice of program content (as discussed in Chapter 5 and in Brislin, 1991). In debate, people are carefully prepared to deal with opponents who take the other side of many controversial issues. Students of debate have to check their emotions when faced with intense disagreements or else they will be downgraded by judges. Further, they have to be well prepared to answer tough questions posed by other debaters who want to impress judges by asking about points for which their opponents have inadequate information and arguments.

BECOMING AN APPRENTICE

After taking a set of courses that are directly or indirectly related to intercultural training, newcomers can gain extremely valuable information by apprenticing themselves to experienced professionals. This can be done during one's college years if there is an international students' office to which one can become attached. Alternatively, students can sometimes become attached to professors who offer intercultural training programs as part of their off-campus consulting activities. Newcomers should keep in mind that there are behaviors that will mark them as good versus bad apprentices. One of us participated in a seminar, organized by the Society for Intercultural Education, Training, and Research (SIETAR), that dealt with advice to newcomers. One experienced professional gave the advice that newcomers must start a reading program and must go well beyond the knowledge they gained through their personal experiences. Of course, this reading program can begin during one's college years as students seek out books and journal articles that go above and beyond assigned readings. This book's reference section provides a good starting point.

In the incident that introduced this chapter, Henry tells Mary that he hasn't taken any courses, demonstrates no evidence of having done much relevant reading, and yet feels that he has a unique perspective to share because he had a German roommate. Although this incident may come across as comical, it is played out again and again in conversations between newcomers and experienced professionals. For some reason not completely understood, people who have had intercultural experiences feel that they can make a living by sharing their conclusions with others. One possibility is that intercultural experiences are so intense, and so challenging to preexisting world views (Chapter 3), that people feel that they have discovered something for the first time! Given their own intensity and enthusiasm, they want to share their discoveries with others. In actuality, trainees are willing to listen to someone else's account of his or her intercultural experiences for about 15 minutes. If these accounts do not move quickly into general principles that the trainees perceive to be relevant, then the training program will be a failure. For example, a trainer might tell a story about a well-meaning clash during his or her Peace Corps assignment in Nepal. If this example does not bring up some general principle about cultural awareness and knowledge (Chapter 2), or deal with emotional confrontations (Chapter 3), or offer guidance for behavior (Chapter 4), and methods for communicating these principles in an interesting way (Chapter 5), then trainees will quickly become bored. The most efficient way of learning about general concepts (that can occasionally and judiciously be explained with the help of one's own experiences) is through the development of an ambitious reading program.

At times, the fact that an apprentice is well read can serve other purposes. Years ago in the American circus, potential workers were expected to offer a variety of skills. There were numerous tasks to be done and circus managers looked for people who could help with many. A contract might read: "play the trumpet in the band, help set up the circus tent, help load wagons for moves from town to town, assist the payroll master with the handling of money, and make oneself generally useful." Apprentices can also strive to make themselves generally useful and at the same time learn about the wide range of issues involved in intercultural training. If newcomers are well read, they can make suggestions about concepts and training methods that may be of use. One of the interesting facts about intercultural training is that newcomers, especially if they have taken relevant courses and have been careful to establish a good reading program, may have a great deal to offer experienced trainers. Experienced people are often so busy with the time-consuming demands of marketing their programs and conducting needs assessment surveys (Chapter 1) that they sometimes fall behind in their professional reading. Apprentices can sometimes fill this gap.

At the SIETAR workshop, another experienced professional (Mitchell Hammer) gave the advice, "Don't be a fizzler." Fizzlers are people who express initial enthusiasm, agree to help with a program, and then drop out upon finding that working hours or job demands are not to their liking. In the incident, Henry's enthusiasm diminished when he discovered that he would have to work evenings and weekends and that he would have to learn to market. He also failed to follow up on his promise to "do anything to help." Fizzlers like Henry not only waste their own time but also contribute to a wariness on the part of experienced professionals who receive phone calls or visits from other potential newcomers.

Another piece of advice is that newcomers should develop additional areas of expertise so that they can eventually offer a variety of training programs. Very few professionals are able to make a living by offering intercultural training programs on a full-time basis. There simply is not yet the demand to support the careers of large numbers of people. The people we know who organize intercultural training programs offer other types of programs as well. For example, we know intercultural trainers who also offer workshops on gender diversity in the workplace, health care delivery, foreign languages, curriculum development at the elementary and secondary school levels, internationalizing the curricula at colleges and universities, basic public speaking skills, basic leadership skills, technical writing, international marketing of products, and so forth. We will return to this recommendation that newcomers learn how to offer a variety of training programs when we discuss "resource development" later in this chapter.

♦ Developing Courses at Colleges and Universities

The number of colleges and universities where courses in intercultural communication are offered has increased over the past 10 years. Colleges and universities react to changes in society and to world events, and these changes include increased intercultural contact both within and between nations. A number of texts have been developed that have been widely adopted. In intercultural communication, for example, books by Gudykunst and Kim (1984), Brislin, Cushner, Cherrie, and Yong (1986), Fontaine (1989) and Samovar and Porter (1991) have proven popular with students and professors. In cross-cultural psychology, texts by Segall, Dasen, Berry, and Poortinga (1990) and Brislin (1993) are available. For a course in international management that draws extensively on work in intercultural communication, books by Hofstede (1980, 1991) and Adler (1991) have proven popular.

To assist in the goal of making intercultural communication a valued part of many universities' curricula, we have been involved in organizing and administering workshops where interested professors have the opportunity to develop new courses. Called "The Summer Workshop for the Development of Intercultural Coursework at Colleges and Universities," the workshop has been offered yearly since 1987 at the East-West Center in Honolulu. Through 1993 the workshops had attracted 290 professors from more than 25 different countries. From our experiences, the following are some of the concerns commonly discussed as professors develop their courses.

The choice of a text has not proven to be a problem. Fortunately, good texts exist (the list above). Perhaps the single biggest issue professors discuss is how best to introduce the concepts "culture" and "communication across cultures." Even though intercultural contact has become increasingly common, there are still large numbers of students who have not had much interaction with people from cultures other than their own. Or, if they think that they have had contact in the past, the interactions may have been so superficial or role-based that no significant learning could possibly have taken place. As an example of role-based interactions, students from the United States who attend seminars organized by a visiting international professor may find themselves in the role of a student interacting with a professor. The role demands associated with behaving like a "good student" may overwhelm any possibility of noticing or learning about cultural differences.

CLASSROOM EXERCISES

The challenge for professors in intercultural courses is to place students in social settings where they actually have to experience cultural differences. This leads to the requirement that professors know how to organize various exercises of the types that we have introduced throughout this book. After introducing the exercise, the professor can then introduce concepts that both help students understand their experiences in the exercise and that introduce research studies that have clarified the concepts. For example, assume that the professor wants to introduce communication differences among people socialized in an individualist versus collectivist culture (Chapter 2). One exercise is to divide students into small groups and have them make decisions about the distribution of resources among people. The exercise can involve the distribution of an unexpected $1,000,000 profit among six workers in an office. Students are told that some of the six workers contributed more than others to the project that eventually led to the $1,000,000 profit. How will the students divide the money? If they read about individualism and collectivism (Hofstede, 1991; Triandis, Brislin, & Hui, 1988) or hear a presentation from their professor, they will learn about the importance of long-term relations among people in a collectivist society. The students will be likely to divide the million dollars on an equal basis: Everyone gets approximately the same amount. They will learn to justify this decision: It is important to give everyone equal amounts so as not to cause ill feelings. In addition, since the people will be together a long time, the workers that contributed less to this project may contribute more to others in the future. Further, if there is disagreement within the group, there will be an emphasis placed on developing win-win solutions that address the needs and opinions of all group members. When they divide the resources among workers socialized in an individualist culture, knowledgeable students will divide on the basis of equity. This means that workers will receive benefits that reflect their individual contributions. If one worker did 40% of the work, he or she will get 40% of the unexpected million dollars.

The important point about this exercise is that it has the purpose of exposing students to important concepts and to making these concepts clearer through the personal involvement of students in their use. At the end of this exercise, students should have significantly more knowledge about five important concepts: individualism, collectivism, equality, equity, and win-win solutions. They should be able to answer test questions about these concepts on traditional midterm and final exams. Understanding a term like *traditional* is very important in the development of college and university courses. Many departments have professors who distrust the use of any exercises and who rely almost exclusively on the lecture format. These professors prepare lectures about various concepts, students take notes and do their assigned readings, and then demonstrate their knowledge on written exams.

These traditional professors often use the phrases "fun and games" or "intellectually lightweight" when discussing classroom exercises in which students participate actively. For some reason, these professors are some of the most powerful and influential within their departments. In addition, they seem to pass by classes where exercises are used just at that moment when students are laughing or having a good time because of their newly found knowledge. For those professors who want to develop intercultural courses and who feel that exercises are valuable in giving students firsthand experiences, we recommend that careful thought be given to the link between exercises and concepts. Exercises must have a clear purpose in the explication of important concepts, and professors should be able to argue that the use of a certain exercise is a better use of classroom time than a straight lecture.

OUT-OF-CLASS EXERCISES

Some professors who have participated in the East-West Center programs (notably Ayse Carden and Renate Mai-Dalton) have shared their experiences with the out-of-class assignments that students have completed. The purpose of these assignments is to give students firsthand experiences interacting with members of another culture. Students then write about their experiences using concepts introduced in class or in their readings. For example, these possibilities are offered to students, and they either choose one or suggest their own equivalent. Admittedly, many of these experiences are more readily available in large cities than in small towns.

- Attending a celebration organized by members of another culture, such as a wedding, coming-of-age ceremony, national or religious celebrations, and so forth.
- Attending meetings of a group of foreign students who meet because of their nationality or a common interest.
- Volunteering to help with the activities of the Foreign Student Advisers' Office or the International Programs Office on campus.
- Visiting a school that people from other nations, or diverse cultural groups within their own country, attend. For example, in many large cities, Japanese nationals send their children to after-hours language schools in which Japanese cultural values are also taught.
- Within these schools, examine the textbooks and especially the introductory reading books to see what lessons are being transmitted to students.
- Spend a day with an international student, allowing him or her to make the decisions about the day's activities.
- Interview an international student concerning a topic about which there are probably large cultural differences. During initial contacts, however, trainees should be cautioned to avoid topics that might put the student on the defensive because many inter-

national students feel that they are representatives of their countries and will therefore be less likely to disclose anything negative or "backwards" about their country. Trainees should ask about less controversial subjects such as how they celebrate their national holidays, what types of food they eat, and how typical teenagers spend their afternoons. If trainees already have a good relationship with an international student, more provocative topics can be covered. The exact topic will depend upon the nationality of the student, but examples would be arranged marriages, governments' relation to press coverage of national events, different markers of distinct social classes within a country, the differential prestige given to various professions, and so forth.

- At a large airport, spend time observing the behavior of people at the arrivals lounge attached to the gates where international flights arrive.
- Visit a social service center where people from various cultural backgrounds are likely to be clients. If professionals at the service center work with many clients from a similar background (e.g., more African Americans or Native Americans than would be expected from the percentage represented in the general population), then ask why these people are overrepresented.
- Many international students have videotapes from their own country or know exactly where they can be found at the local Blockbuster Video store. Talk to one of these students about what videotapes might be borrowed or rented to expand one's view about another country, and why the international student makes his or her recommendations.
- Students with a background in music might collect a set of children's songs, or work songs, from another culture.
- Dine at a number of ethnic restaurants within the community.

The "ethnic restaurant" recommendation needs expansion since it is so frequently seen as unnecessary given the widespread belief that many students already patronize these establishments. Returning to our discussion of skeptical professors who see little use for in- or out-of-class exercises, the written reports prepared by students that are mistakenly placed in their mailboxes will surely describe restaurant visits. Our experience has been that beliefs about frequent student patronization are simply wrong. Many students have not visited ethnic restaurants in their community and find it very interesting and impactful when asked to do so as a class project. One of our colleagues who teaches in New Jersey takes his intercultural communication students on a field trip to restaurants in New York City, especially in Chinatown and Little Italy. He is constantly surprised that his students who have lived in New York report seeing these places for the first time.

In a recent study, the number of visits to various ethnic restaurants was found to be significantly correlated with intercultural sensitivity (Bhawuk & Brislin, 1992). The interpretation of this result (consistent with the discussion of "openness to experience" by Paunonen, Jackson, Trzebinski, & Fosterling, 1992) is that the act of visiting ethnic restaurants reflects the willingness to change one's typical behaviors (Chapter 4). When the different experiences bring positive results and are stimulating but not overwhelming, people modify (however slightly) their previous attitudes that placed limits on the types of behaviors in which they would engage. Their general attitude concerning openness to new experiences changes, and the willingness to interact frequently with people from other cultural backgrounds is one example of this newly developed openness. Our recommendation, then, is that visits to ethnic restaurants should not be dismissed as a class activity. In its application, students find such visits mind-opening and impactful.

◆ Developing Sophistication About the Uses of Power

When college professors realize that there can be objections to in-class and out-of-class exercises and when they take steps to defuse these criticisms, they are demonstrating a sophistication concerning the importance of power. Our major argument in this section is that if all professionals interested in intercultural training become more knowledgeable about power, their work will be easier. One of us prepared an extensive treatment concerning power's role in people's lives (Brislin, 1991), and much of this material is an expansion of themes presented in that book.

Power refers to the total set of resources a person can put forward such that his or her recommendations and decisions are implemented. *Decisions* is used broadly, and it can include the decision to accept a job should it be offered, the decision to spend money in a certain way, or the decision to hire certain staff members. Many people make recommendations and communicate their clear preferences that a certain decision be made. Far fewer people's recommendations are listened to, and far fewer people have their decisions taken seriously. The people who are listened to and taken seriously are said to have power.

COMPETITION FOR RESOURCES

Intercultural trainers need to become sophisticated about power because they are competing for resources with others who are just as smart, hardworking, and well-intentioned. Take the example of intercultural training programs that might be offered in a number of organizations. Resources include money, the time that trainees might take off from their work, personnel for the training staff, the limited attention of high-level executives, space within the organization where training might be held, and so forth. One of the most shocking facts newcomers face is that others in the organization prefer that resources be expended on projects other than intercultural training. For example, assume that trainers have proposed a very good program that they argue will prepare people for the challenges of their future intercultural interactions. The proposed budget is modest, and yet it represents a potential investment of resources that would not be available for some other project. Consider the possible responses of their colleagues within a number of organizations:

a. Colleagues in an international student advisers' office may prefer that the money be spent on a training program so that all office staff will understand visas and visa regulations.

b. Colleagues in a small business may prefer that training be offered in the uses of a recent computer software project aimed at improving financial forecasting.
c. Colleagues in a social service agency may prefer that money be spent on child care for working parents.
d. Colleagues in a counseling center may feel that the money will be better spent on a program that integrates the efforts of volunteer paraprofessionals.
e. Colleagues in a school system may argue that money will be better spent on acquiring needed textbooks and materials.

Intercultural trainers will often find that all of these alternative uses of resources are reasonable. None can be dismissed as the proposals of insensitive and ignorant people. Even though a common response of intercultural trainers is to argue immediately that their training programs are more valuable than these other proposals, this is usually an unwise response. It is easy for intercultural trainers to communicate a "holier than thou" attitude and to look down their noses at others who are "not as interculturally sophisticated as we are." A far better response is to become more sophisticated about power and to compete wisely for resources within one's organization. Although space limitations prevent an extensive treatment (more information is available in Brislin, 1991), the following recommendations provide examples of steps that intercultural trainers can take.

RESOURCE DEVELOPMENT AND EXCHANGE

If newcomers to training take the advice presented earlier in this chapter, they will develop a number of resources above and beyond their interests in intercultural communication. For example, they can become good public speakers, good writers, and good leaders of group discussions. They can also become knowledgeable about technical areas such as accounting, finance, statistics, health care delivery, curriculum development, and so forth. With these resources, these newcomers can then make themselves useful within their organizations. Instead of arguing against the very reasonable, worthwhile projects of others, they can help those others achieve their goals. Later, the newcomers can ask these others for various types of help in the development of intercultural training. This mutual giving of favors, or exchange of resources (Cialdini, 1988), is central to project development in organizations. While mythology may extol the virtues of the person acting alone and the person who can solve problems by himself or herself, reality is different. Intercultural training demands the talents of many people, and if newcomers can offer their talents to others and can earn their gratitude, the newcomers can expect help at a later date.

DEVELOPING A NETWORK OF INFLUENTIAL PEOPLE

People who are sophisticated about power offer their resources to others so that favors might be returned at a later time. Where do these people meet others who might engage in this mutual give and take of favors? The answer is that people should engage in the set of activities that has come to be known as "networking." The term is frequently heard among intercultural trainers. In workshops aimed at assisting newcomers who want to enter the field (e.g., the workshop sponsored by SIETAR, described previously), the advice to start networks was given by several experienced professionals.

In these same workshops, the following questions might be asked:

1. Think of people with whom you share the major emotional experiences of your lives. Your successful experiences are shared by them, and vice-versa. Their disappointments are shared by you. How many such people are there in your life right now?
2. How many people are there that you know whom you can approach without being introduced, perhaps call them by their first name (although this element depends on cultural norms), and ask them for information on one or more topics?
3. Think of people with whom you interacted frequently in the past (within about the past 10 years), but with whom you interact far less frequently now. Why has the interaction decreased? Try to think of people for whom the answer is not simply that you (or

the other person) moved a long distance to another city or country.

When the answers to these questions are compared among newcomers, people rarely report a number greater than 20 in response to the first question. What is a good term for these 20 or fewer people? Most workshop members suggest that "close friends" is a good choice. These same workshop participants often report, in response to the second question, that they can identify upwards of 100 people. What is the best term for these people? After entertaining possibilities such as "casual friends," "acquaintances," and "colleagues," some participants agree that "members of my network" is also a possibility.

People in networks exchange favors with each other (Triandis, Brislin, & Hui, 1988). For example, Person A hears about a job opening and gives this information to Person B. Later, Person B volunteers some of his or her free time and gives a presentation in Person A's training program. These two people are not necessarily close friends. They may become friends in the future, but the mutual giving and receiving of favors is not dependent upon friendship. It is important that people in networks make sure that they are giving sufficient attention to returning the favors that they have received. If they do not, they will find themselves dropped from network membership and may even find that they have developed the reputation of being "users," "takers," or "leeches." In response to the third question, above, some workshop participants identify the absence of returned favors as a reason for the cessation of relationships. For example, they report, "This other person always expected me to be there when I was needed for something. But this person was never around when I needed some help."

Workshops for newcomers can include recommendations for developing networks. One way is to join community organizations that have influential people as members. In communities that we know, these organizations include the Symphony Orchestra support group, the Blood Bank, docents for museum tours, political parties, university alumni associations, volunteer groups for overseas student exchange programs, and so forth. When newcomers make themselves generally useful to these organizations by volunteering their services for various committees, they will meet others who may be able to help them at a later date. Another way to become involved in networks is to examine one's interests. Whether people play bridge, chess, backgammon, tennis, or a musical instrument, they can often find a club that appeals to any of these interests. Or a person might be competent at some sport and may also enjoy working with young people. There are many community organizations for the support of youth baseball, softball, soccer, football, and basketball that are looking for coaches. Many physicians, lawyers, businesspeople, and university professors will be met when parents drop off and pick up their children at the practice site.

For newcomers to intercultural training, networks should also be established through membership organizations such as the Society for Intercultural Education, Training, and Research and/or the American Society for Training and Development. If people come to intercultural training with a strong background in one of the academic disciplines, they might also consider joining international organizations such as the International Association for Cross-Cultural Psychology, the Society for Cross-Cultural Research (many anthropologists, sociologists, and psychologists are members), the intercultural communication division of the International Communication Association, or the Academy of International Business.

While recognizing the wisdom of all this advice, some newcomers are sure to have a question such as the following. "This all sounds fine for people who meet others easily and who are comfortable in new social situations. They can join various organizations and meet others quickly. But I am shy and am not at ease in new social situations. What can I do?" There are two answers. One is that networking becomes easier the more it is done. The other answer is that newcomers can immediately seek out a role in the volunteer organization they want to join. They might do some homework and find out what jobs organizational leaders have a hard time filling. For example, many leaders have a difficult time finding people willing to edit or write for their organizations' newsletters. If newcomers can volunteer for this task, they will be welcomed. Then, the newcomers can approach others in the role of a writer for the newsletter. Because almost all organization members enjoy seeing their names in print, they will be happy to talk to the newsletter representative. Other roles that allow easy interaction with others include member of the finance committee ("How do you think money should be spent this year?"), program committee ("Who might be a good speaker at upcoming meetings?"), and community outreach committee ("What other people in our community should know of our work or receive our newsletter?"). Answers to this last question, of course, permit even more opportunities for networking.

DEVELOPING THE IMAGE OF A WINNER

If newcomers invest their time, energy, and abilities in the activities of community organizations, they should develop reputations as hard workers who can accomplish important tasks. Eventually, members of the organization will recognize the newcomers' contributions and will make a point of returning favors. The members might inform the newcomers about a potential job opening that could include organizations involved in international activities. Whenever they have the opportunities to show their talents either in the volunteer organization or in activities more closely related to their professional goals, newcomers should consider the strategy known as "small wins" (Weick, 1984).

Everybody loves winners and wants to be associated with them. People also are more likely to offer jobs or contracts to newcomers who have the image of being winners. One way to develop this image is to formulate goals that can surely be attained. If goals are set and attained often enough, others will notice and will conclude that the newcomers are winners who are successful in what they try to do. At times, developing the image of a winner means that newcomers have to understand human nature.

Assume that two newcomers, through their networks, gain permission to offer an intercultural communication workshop in an organization. As will often be the case when they make their first commitment to intercultural training, executives will allow employees to attend on an after-hours and voluntary basis. That is, employees can participate in training, but during an evening session or on a Saturday. Naturally, not all employees will be able to attend the program. Trainers will be asked to estimate the number of employees who will voluntarily come. Here is where an interesting fact about human nature plays a part. If trainers estimate that 10 people will come and 15 actually show up, then they are winners! They give programs that are so attractive that employees will voluntarily come! But if the trainers had estimated that 20 people will come and the same 15 show up, then they are losers! The trainers will be seen an unexciting drones who can't deliver on their promises!

We once gave advice to people that was based on the same underlying idea of sensitivity to human nature. Some graduate students were planning a workshop that had never been offered before. They wanted our help in reserving a room. Our advice was to reserve one of the smaller rooms that was available. We argued that if 30 people showed up in a room where 60 could be comfortably seated, then the room would seem bare and observers might conclude that the workshop was a failure. But if the 30 people showed up in a room where 25 could be seated comfortably, then observers would conclude that the workshop must be generating a lot of interest.

The general recommendation, then, is to think about projects in terms of goals that can surely be accomplished. Complex projects sometimes have to be broken down into a set of attainable goals. Once an early goal is attained, the prediction is that others will look at the project leaders as winners. Some of these others will then want to join the project team, and consequently there will be more people available to work toward the next attainable goal.

◆ Long-Range Planning

Just as networking becomes easier the longer people do it, efforts to develop intercultural programs proceed more smoothly the longer trainers demonstrate the usefulness of their work. When they first accept positions in an organization or accept contracts as outside consultants, intercultural trainers often face bewilderment on the part of organizational personnel. Concepts such as "special adjustment problems on overseas assignments," "cultural differences in communication," and "adjusting behaviors to be more effective in other cultures" are still foreign to many people. In our experiences, this bewilderment will last for about 2 years. Most people have not had intercultural experiences that were impactful enough to help them understand the nature of culture, cultural differences, ethnocentrism, ethnorelativism, and so forth. Yet if trainers enter organizations, make themselves useful to others, develop good programs, graduate "alumni" of the programs who talk enthusiastically about their experiences, and demonstrate the positive effects of their programs through good evaluation studies over a 2-year period, then they will be able to count on continued organizational support. The trainers will find that executives say, "Of course we must have intercultural communication training. There are special demands when our employees work in other cultures. We must support them, and we must also remain competitive with other organizations, through good training programs."

◆ The Timing of Programs

When trainers have earned the trust and confidence of executives, they can begin to develop programs that support the organization's personnel throughout their intercultural assignments. They can go beyond predeparture training, or programs held just prior to people's intercultural assignments, and can plan activities that provide long-term support. Two possibilities are mid-assignment programs and reentry workshops before people return to their own countries.

Midterm programs, or any programs that take place a month or more after people accept intercultural assignments, take advantage of the fact that people will have encountered intercultural differences and will want to discuss them (Gudykunst & Hammer, 1983). In sharp contrast to predeparture programs, which cannot be developed on the assumption that trainees know what intercultural experiences are, midterm programs can take advantage of trainees' experiences. Even if they are only a month into their assignments, all trainees have had interactions with culturally diverse co-workers and will have had experiences that they do not completely understand. Trainees will be eager to discuss these and will look forward to help in interpreting and understanding the experiences. Gudykunst and Hammer (1983) suggest that there is a sharp distinction in the needs trainees experience as a function of time. Just before and just after the start of their intercultural experience, trainees want survival information. If their assignment is in another country, they will want information on housing, food, and transportation. If the intercultural interactions are to be in their own country, they will want to know about the changes in their lives they can expect once they interact more frequently across cultural boundaries. But once people learn that they can survive in the other country and can make basic adjustments to the needs of people from diverse cultures, they want more advanced information on intercultural communication. They want to understand why cultural differences exist and may be willing to make certain adjustments in their everyday behaviors as long as they understand the reasons why the new behaviors are more appropriate. They become more than willing to entertain the quite sophisticated thought that they will be more effective if they take cultural differences into account.

Midterm programs can also encourage or reinforce the development of support groups (Adelman, 1988). For example, Arnold (1967) was concerned that many Peace Corps volunteers in certain South American countries were returning home prior to the completion of their assignments. Noting that volunteers were making the decision to return home about 6 months into their assignments, he established a midterm training program at about this point when volunteer enthusiasm was obviously low. Trainees came together and discussed their problems, shared difficulties brought on by culture shock, asked for interpretations of cultural differences they had observed, and reinforced each other for successes. Arnold found that after this program, the premature return rate of participants was only 25% of that found among Peace Corps volunteers on similar assignments who had not participated in a midterm program.

Another point at which beneficial programs can be offered occurs just before or just after sojourners are to return to their own culture. Many people report that the culture shock they faced upon returning to their own country was greater than the initial shock of adjusting to the other culture. Even though they admit that they probably would have turned down an opportunity to participate, they are convinced that a reentry program would have been beneficial. There is now an extensive literature on reentry shock and programs to deal with it (Austin, 1986; LaBrack, 1985; Martin, 1986; Uehara, 1986), and people who participate find the programs valuable. The most difficult aspect of organizing such programs, however, is to persuade potential participants to come. The idea that people will have difficulty readjusting to their own culture is simply not a thought that they entertain. In fact, they find it absurd and find it difficult to talk to trainers without laughing. In addition, a reentry seminar faces competition with other activities such as packing for the move home, saying goodbye to friends, buying gifts for people back home, and so forth. People begin to experience reentry shock (recall the diagram in Chapter 3) a few months after returning home. Unless they are working for an organization where the trainers have established the concept that all returnees should participate in reentry programs, people will not have easy access to various kinds of support that will help them deal with readjustment to their own culture.

One of the factors that makes reentry so difficult is that during their sojourns many people use images of their home countries to help them cope with difficulties. They assure and reassure themselves that the problems they are encountering will disappear once they go back home. As a result, many have an idealized vision of their home countries and an unrealistic expectation of how wonderful life will be when they return home. As discussed in Chapter 2, the larger the gap between people's expectations and reality, the greater the stress that is experienced. Helping trainees create a more realistic perspective on returning home is, therefore, essential in reducing reentry shock.

Once they begin to experience reverse culture shock, returnees frequently complain that they expected old friends to be interested in hearing about their intercultural experiences. People know they have changed, know that they have had life-changing experiences, and know that they have developed a more international outlook. Returnees are severely disappointed when they find that old friends are willing to listen politely for about one-half hour but then change the subject to topics such as local sports, national politics, or their current hobbies. Another emotional reaction is that returnees don't know exactly how to behave given the changes in themselves that they recognize. They don't know how to continue their intercultural and international interests and don't know how to deal with their seemingly uninterested friends. One of many possible responses to their frustration is anger, and so returnees sometimes lash out at friends and colleagues. Such a response, of course, contributes to the distancing between returnees and old friends.

Other problems returnees frequently report occur in the workplace. One fact about overseas assignments is that people are usually far away from the home office of their organization. People frequently report that they have far more latitude in their decision making, and report directly to fewer superiors, while on overseas assignments. Upon returning home, however, they find themselves in the company of many superiors who want to approve or disapprove people's recommendations. The returnees are especially frustrated when they have to deal with superiors who want final decision-making authority but who have far less knowledge about a specific policy initiative. Another issue about which returnees sometimes complain is that their overseas experience is not as valued as other types of contributions when executives make decisions about promotions. At times, people accept overseas assignments only to find that, upon their return, individuals who used to be their subordinates are now their superiors.

Sojourners who were especially successful because they modified their behaviors to meet cultural expectation (Chapter 4) can face especially impactful reverse culture shock experiences. One businessperson we know was especially successful in Asia because he carried out his dealings in the Asian manner: building trust, communicating that he would always be present to deal with problems without calling in lawyers, patience, attention to quality control, looking after unimaginative but loyal employees, looking at issues over the long term and not being tempted by short-term profits, and so forth. Returning to the United States after 15 years in Asia, he was literally shocked to find how little could be done without the continual involvement of lawyers and how long-term planning was stymied by the emphasis placed on quarterly reports. For another example, recall Fakir from India (in the incident that introduced Chapter 1). If successful in his graduate studies in the United States, he would learn to make his own decisions. If he was a student of English Literature, for example, he would be expected to formulate his own interpretations of poems, plays, and novels. Upon returning to India, he might expect the same of his students. Indian returnees have told us, however, that students respond as follows: "You're the professor! You tell us what the interpretation of this poem is!" Among themselves, the students will gripe, "If he doesn't know what the poem means, he doesn't deserve to hold down the post of professor!"

Good reentry programs (a number of models are available in Austin, 1986) can assist returnees to deal with these challenges. Although admittedly difficult to establish, they can be most valuable to the work of trainers as they attempt to establish positive long-term relations with organizations. The reason is that returnees will be a constant presence in the organization. If they are enthusiastic about the value of reentry programs, they will communicate this to coworkers and to executives. If they put their positive experiences with the reentry program together with the benefits of their predeparture and midterm training, they will be supporters of the goal to make training programs a normal and expected part of people's intercultural assignments.

◆ Some Final Thoughts

Much of this chapter has been concerned with how newcomers can best prepare themselves to make a living, or to supplement their income in a meaningful way, as intercultural trainers. We have recommended the careful selection of college courses, the establishment of a long-term reading program, apprenticeships with experienced professionals, the development of sophistication concerning power, and the nurturance of wide networks. These steps in career development will have a number of positive outcomes. They will allow potential trainers to develop and to market a number of different programs to meet the needs of various organizations. Once programs start, the knowledge and skills trainers develop allow them to answer a wide variety of questions. The ability to answer diverse questions, and to engage trainees in discussions of issues, is central to executives' decisions whether to invite the trainers back or not.

The knowledge and skills developed also allow trainers to be flexible in their careers. The organization of intercultural programs often entails a great deal of travel, especially as trainers organize programs to be held after sojourners begin their overseas assignments. While romantic and exciting at first, there can come a time in people's careers when they find that (a) they do not want to see the inside of any more jet planes or hotel rooms and (b) they want to see their children's school recitals instead of missing them because of job assignments. A wide variety of skills allows people to choose among many career opportunities, and they allow people to request job flexibility so that they can accept intercultural training assignments that are close to home.

Finally, people with extensive knowledge and multiple skills bring credit to the field of intercultural training. Too often in the past, intercultural programs have been organized by people whose only credentials were that they once had some intercultural experiences. While this allowed them to give a presentation in one session within a workshop, personal experiences alone do not prepare trainers to organize a variety of good sessions and to answer the many questions that trainees have. As a result of their observations of such trainers, many potential clients do not have a high opinion of intercultural training. If trainers develop their knowledge base and skills and are able to communicate their competencies given their wide networks, the reputation of intercultural training will increase given the clear capabilities of the professionals it attracts.

References

Adelman, M. (1988). Cross-cultural adjustment. A theoretical perspective on social support. *International Journal of Intercultural Relations, 12,* 183-204.

Adelman, M., & Lustig, M. (1981). Intercultural communication problems as perceived by Saudi Arabian and American managers. *International Journal of Intercultural Relations, 5,* 349-363.

Adler, N. (1991). *International dimensions of organizational behavior* (2nd ed.). Boston: PWS-Kent.

Albert, M. (1985). Assessing cultural change needs. *Training and Development Journal, 39*(5), 94-98.

Albert, R., & Adamopoulos, J. (1980). An attributional approach to culture learning: The culture assimilator. In M. Hamnett & R. W. Brislin (Eds.), *Research in culture learning: Language and conceptual studies* (pp. 53-60). Honolulu: University Press of Hawaii.

Althen, G. (1984). *The handbook of foreign student advising.* Yarmouth, ME: Intercultural Press.

Aranda, L. (1986). International trading: Programs for success. *Training and Development Journal, 40*(4), 71-73.

Arnold, C. (1967). Culture shock and a Peace Corps field mental health program. *Community Mental Health Journal, 3,* 53-60.

Aronson, E. (1972). *The social animal.* San Francisco: Freeman.

Austin, C. (Ed.). (1986). *Cross-cultural reentry: A book of readings.* Abilene, TX: Abilene Christian University.

Barna, L. M. (1983). The stress factor in intercultural relations. In D. Landis & R. Brislin (Eds.), *The handbook of intercultural training* (Vol. 2, pp. 19-49). Elmsford, NY: Pergamon.

Barnes, R. L. (1985). Across cultures: The Peace Corps training model. *Training and Development Journal, 39*(10), 46-49.

Barnlund, D. C., & Yoshioka, M. (1990). Apologies: Japanese and American styles. *International Journal of Intercultural Relations, 14,* 193-206.

Befus, C. (1988). A multilevel approach for culture shock experienced by sojourners. *International Journal of Intercultural Relations, 12,* 381-400.

Bellah, R. N., Madsen, R., Sullivan, W. M., Swindler, A., & Tipton, S. M. (1985). *Habits of the heart: Individualism and commitment in American life*. Berkeley: University of California Press.

Bennett, J. (1986). Modes of cross-cultural training: Conceptualizing cross-cultural training as education. *International Journal of Intercultural Relations, 10,* 117-134.

Bennett, M. (1991). New insights for intercultural sensitivity model. *Training and Culture Journal, 3*(5), 5.

Bennett, M. J. (1986). A developmental approach to training for intercultural sensitivity. *International Journal of Intercultural Relations, 10,* 179-196.

Bergsgaard, M., & Larsonn, E. (1984). Increasing social interaction between an isolate first grader and cross-cultural peers. *Psychology in the Schools, 21,* 244-251.

Berk, R., & Rossi, P. (1990). *Thinking about program evaluation*. Newbury Park, CA: Sage.

Berry, E., Kessler, J., Fodor, J., & Wato, W. (1983). Intercultural communication for health personnel. *International Journal of Intercultural Relations, 7,* 377-392.

Berry, J. W. (1990). Psychology of acculturation: Understanding individuals moving between cultures. In R. Brislin (Ed.), *Applied cross-cultural psychology* (pp. 232-253). Newbury Park, CA: Sage.

Berryman-Fink, C., & Fink, C. (1985). Optimal training for opposite-sex managers. *Training and Development Journal, 39*(2), 27-29.

Bhawuk, D. P. S. (1990). Cross-cultural orientation programs. In R. Brislin (Ed.), *Applied cross-cultural psychology* (pp. 325-346). Newbury Park, CA: Sage.

Bhawuk, D. P. S., & Brislin, R. (1992). The measurement of intercultural sensitivity using the concepts of individualism and collectivism. *International Journal of Intercultural Relations, 16,* 413-436.

Birnbrauer, H. (1987). Trouble-shooting your training program. *Training and Development Journal, 41*(9), 18-20.

Black, J. S., & Mendenthall, M. (1990). Cross-cultural training effectiveness: A review and a theoretical framework for future research. *Academy of Management Review, 15,* 113-136.

Bogorya, Y. (1985). Intercultural training for managers involved in international business. *Journal of Management Development, 4*(2), 17-25.

Brislin, R. (1981). *Cross-cultural encounters: Face-to-face encounters*. Elmsford, NY: Pergamon.

Brislin, R. (1989). Intercultural communication training. In M. Asante & W. Gudykunst (Eds.), *Handbook of international and intercultural communication* (pp. 441-457). Newbury Park, CA: Sage.

Brislin, R. (1991). *The art of getting things done: A practical guide to the use of power*. New York: Praeger.

Brislin, R. (1993). *Understanding culture's influence on behavior*. Fort Worth, TX: Harcourt Brace Jovanovich.

Brislin, R., Cushner, K., Cherrie, C., & Yong, M. (1986). *Intercultural interactions: A practical guide*. Newbury Park, CA: Sage.

Brislin, R., Landis, D., & Brandt, M. (1983). Conceptualization of intercultural behavior and training. In D. Landis & R. Brislin (Eds.), *Handbook of intercultural training* (Vol. 1, pp. 1-35). Elmsford, NY: Pergamon.

Brislin, R., & Pedersen, P. (1976). *Cross-cultural orientation programs*. New York: Gardner Press.

Brislin, R., & Takaki, T. (1992). The advantages of a conceptual approach to the analysis of intercultural interactions. In T. Hilgers, M. Wunsch, & V. Chattergy (Eds.), *Academic literacies in multicultural higher education* (pp. 70-78). Honolulu: University of Hawaii, Center for Studies of Multicultural Higher Education.

Brislin, R., & Yoshida, T. (Eds.). (1994). *Improving intercultural interactions: Modules for cross-cultural training programs*. Thousand Oaks, CA: Sage.

Broaddus, D. (1986). *Use of the Culture General Assimilator in intercultural training*. Unpublished doctoral dissertation, Indiana State University, Terre Haute.

Buchanan, K. (1990). Vocational English-as-a-second language programs. *ERIC Digest* (ED 321551).

Bussom, R., Elsaid, H., Schermerhorn, J., & Wilson, H. (1984). Integrated management-organization development in a developing country: A case study. *Journal of Management Development, 3*(1), 3-15.

Budner, S. (1962). Intolerance of ambiguity as a personality variable. *Journal of Personality, 30*(1), 29-50.

Campbell, D., & Stanley, J. (1966). *Experimental and quasi-experimental designs for research*. Chicago: Rand-McNally.

Carbaugh, D. (Ed.). (1990). *Cultural communication and intercultural contact*. Hillsdale, NJ: Lawrence Erlbaum.

Carey, J., Reinart, M., & Fontes, L. (1990). School counselor's perceptions of training needs in multicultural counseling. *Counselor Education and Supervision, 29*(3), 155-169.

Center for Applied Linguistics (1982). *Providing effective cultural orientation: A training guide*. Washington, DC: Center for Applied Linguistics. (ERIC Document Reproduction Service No. ED 218985).

Charlesworth, E., Williams, B., & Baer, P. (1984). Stress management at the workshop: Compliance, cost-benefit, health care and hypertension-related variables. *Psychosomatic Medicine, 46*, 387-397.

Chinese Culture Connection. (1987). Chinese values and the search for culture-free dimensions of culture. *Journal of Cross-Cultural Psychology, 18*, 143-164.

Cialdini, R. (1988). *Influence: Science and practice*. Glenview, IL: Scott-Foresman.

Cogswell, D., & Stubblefield, H. (1988). Assessing the training and staff development needs of mental health professionals. *Administration and Policy in Mental Health, 16*(1), 14-24.

Collett, P. (1971). Training Englishmen in the non-verbal behaviour of Arabs: An experiment on intercultural communication. *International Journal of Psychology, 6*(3), 209-215.

Collier, M. J., Ribeau, S. A., & Hecht, M. (1986). Intercultural communication rules and outcomes within three domestic cultures. *International Journal of Intercultural Relations, 10,* 439-457.

Cook, T., Campbell, D., & Peracchio, L. (1991). Quasi-experiments. In M. Dunette & L. Hough (Eds.), *Handbook of industrial and organizational psychology* (2nd ed.) (Vol. 2, pp. 491-576). Palo Alto, CA: Consulting Psychologists Press.

Copeland, L., & Griggs, L. (1985). *Going international: How to make friends and deal effectively in the global marketplace.* New York: Random House.

Cushner, K. (1989). Assessing the impact of a culture-general assimilator. *International Journal of Intercultural Relations, 13,* 125-146.

Davidson, G., Hansford, B., & Moriarty, B. (1983). Interpersonal apprehension and cultural majority-minority miscommunication. *Australian Psychologist, 18,* 97-105.

Day, N. (1990). Training providers to serve culturally different AIDS patients. *Family and Community Health, 13*(2), 46-53.

Deal, T. E., & Kennedy, A. A. (1982). *Corporate cultures: The rites and rituals of corporate life.* Reading, MA: Addison-Wesley.

Detweiler, R. (1980). Intercultural interaction and the categorization process: A conceptual analysis and behavioral outcome. *International Journal of Intercultural Relations, 4,* 275-293.

Dixon, N. (1987). Meet training's goals without reaction forms. *Personnel Journal, 66*(8), 108-115.

Dotlich, D. (1982). International and intercultural management development. *Training and Development Journal, 36*(10), 26-31.

Earley, P. C. (1987). Intercultural training for managers: A comparison of documentary and interpersonal methods. *Academy of Management Journal, 30,* 685-698.

Esquivel, G., & Keitel, M. (1990). Counseling immigrant children in the schools. *Elementary School Guidance and Counseling, 24*(3), 213-221.

Everts, J. (1988). The Marae-based Hui: Intensive induction to cross-cultural counselling, a New Zealand experiment. *International Journal for the Advancement of Counselling, 11,* 97-104.

Fantini, A. E. (Ed.). (1984). Getting the whole picture: A student's field guide to language acquisition and culture exploration. *International Exchange Series.* Washington, DC: U.S.I.A.

Fiedler, F., Mitchell, T., & Triandis, H. (1971). The culture assimilator: An approach to cross-cultural training. *Journal of Applied Psychology, 55,* 95-102.

Fisher, R., & Price, L. (1991). International pleasure travel and post-vacation cultural change. *Journal of Leisure Research, 23*(3), 193-208.

Fontaine, G. (1986). Roles of social support systems in overseas relocation: Implications for intercultural training. *International Journal of Intercultural Relations, 10,* 361-378.

Fontaine, G. (1989). *Managing international assignment: The strategy for success.* Englewood Cliffs, NJ: Prentice Hall.

Friday, R. A. (1989). Contrasts in discussion behaviors of German and American managers. *International Journal of Intercultural Relations, 13,* 429-446.

Furnham, A., & Bochner, S. (1986). *Culture shock: Psychological reactions to unfamiliar environments*. London: Methuen.

Ganster, D., Mayes, B., Sime, W., & Tharp, G. (1982). Managing organizational stress: A field experiment. *Journal of Applied Psychology, 67*, 533-542.

Gao, G., & Gudykunst, W. (1990). Uncertainty, anxiety, and adaptation. *International Journal of Intercultural Relations, 14*, 301-317.

Gim, R., Atkinson, D., & Kim, S. (1991). Asian-American acculturation, counselor ethnicity and cultural sensitivity, and ratings of counselors. *Journal of Counseling Psychology, 38*, 57-62.

Goldstein, A. P. (1988). *The prepare curriculum: Teaching prosocial competencies*. Champaign, IL: Research Press.

Goldstein, I. (1991). Training in work organizations. In M. Dunnette & L. Hough (Eds.), *Handbook of industrial and organizational psychology* (2nd ed.) (Vol. 2, pp. 507-619). Palo Alto, CA: Consulting Psychologists Press.

Gonzalez, G. (1985). InterAmerican and intercultural education and the Chicano community. *The Journal of Ethnic Studies, 13*, 31-53.

Goodnow, C. (1992, June 15). Friends for life: Amigos training dispenses a big dose of reality. *Seattle Post-Intelligence*, pp. C1-C2.

Gudykunst, W. (Ed.). (1986). *Intergroup communication*. London: Edward Arnold.

Gudykunst, W., & Hammer, M. (1983). Basic training design: Approaches to intercultural training. In D. Landis & R. Brislin (Eds.), *Handbook of intercultural training: Vol. 1. Issues in theory and design* (pp. 118-154). Elmsford, NY: Pergamon.

Gudykunst, W., & Hammer, M. (1984). Dimensions of intercultural effectiveness: Culture specific or culture general? *International Journal of Intercultural Relations, 8*, 1-10.

Gudykunst, W., Hammer, M., & Wiseman, R. (1977). An analysis of an integrated approach to cross-cultural training. *International Journal of Intercultural Relations, 1*, 99-110.

Gudykunst, W., & Kim, Y. (1984). *Communicating with strangers: An approach to intercultural communication*. New York: Random House.

Gullahorn, J., & Gullahorn, J. (1963). An extension of the U-curve hypothesis. *Journal of Social Issues, 19*(3), 33-47.

Guttentag, M., & Struening, E. (Eds). (1975). *Handbook of evaluation research* (2 vols.). Beverly Hills, CA: Sage.

Hall, E. T. (1983). *Hidden differences: Studies in international communication—How to communicate with the Germans*. Hamburg, West Germany: Stern Magazine Gruner + Jahr AG & Co.

Hammer, M. (1989). Intercultural communication competence. In M. Asante & W. Gudykunst (Eds.), *Handbook of international and intercultural communication* (pp. 247-260). Newbury Park, CA: Sage.

Harman, R., & Briggs, N. (1991). SIETAR survey: Perceived contributions of the social sciences to intercultural communication. *International Journal of Intercultural Relations, 15*, 19-28.

Harper, F. (1973). What counselors must know about the social sciences of black Americans. *Journal of Negro Education, 42*, 109-116.

Harris, P. R., & Moran, R. T. (1979). *Managing cultural differences.* Houston: Gulf Publishing.

Harris, P. R., & Moran, R. T. (1987). *Managing cultural differences* (2nd ed.). Houston: Gulf Publishing.

Hawes, F., & Kealey, D. J. (1981). An empirical study of Canadian technical assistance. *International Journal of Intercultural Relations, 5,* 239-258.

Heath, A., Neimeyer, G., & Pedersen, P. (1988). The future of cross-cultural counseling: A Delphi poll. *Journal of Counseling and Development, 67,* 27-30.

Hecht, M. L., & Ribeau, S. (1984). Ethnic communication: A comparative analysis of satisfying communication. *International Journal of Intercultural Relations, 8,* 135-151.

Henderson, G. (1979). *Understanding and counseling ethnic minorities.* Springfield, IL: Charles C Thomas.

Hofstede, G. (1980). *Culture's consequences: International differences in work-related values.* Beverly Hills, CA: Sage.

Hofstede, G. (1986). Cultural differences in teaching and learning. *International Journal of Intercultural Relations, 10,* 301-320.

Hofstede, G. (1991). *Cultures and organizations: Software of the mind.* London: McGraw-Hill.

Hofstede, G., & Bond, M. (1988). Confucius & economic growth: New trends in culture's consequences. *Organizational Dynamics, 16*(4), 4-21.

Holmes, T. H., & Rahe, R. H. (1967). The social readjustment scale. *Journal of Psychosomatic Research, 2,* 216.

House, J. S. (1985). Barriers to work stress: I. Social support. In W. D. Gentry, H. Benson, & C. J. deWolff (Eds.), *Behavioral medicine: Work, stress and health* (pp. 157-178). Dordrecht, Netherlands: Martinus Nijhoff.

Ilola, L. (1989). *Intercultural interaction training for preservice teachers using the culture-general assimilator with a peer interactive approach.* Doctoral Dissertation, University of Hawaii.

Ilola, L. (1990). Culture and health. In R. Brislin (Ed.), Applied cross-cultural psychology (pp. 278-301). Newbury Park, CA: Sage.

Inman, M. (1985). Language and cross-cultural training in American multinational corporations. *Modern Language Journal, 69,* 247-255.

Johnson, D. (1989). The Houston Parent-Child Development Center project: Disseminating a viable program for enhancing at-risk families. *Prevention in Human Services, 7*(1), 89-108.

Jones, R. (1983). Increasing staff sensitivity to black clients. *Social Casework, 64,* 419-425.

Kaplan, R. B. (1966). Cultural thought patterns and inter-cultural education. *Language Learning, 16*(1-2), 1-20.

Katz, D. (1960). The functional approach to the study of attitudes. *Public Opinion Quarterly, 24,* 164-204.

Katz, J. (1977). The effects of a systematic training program on the attitudes and behaviors of white people. *International Journal of Intercultural Relations, 1,* 77-89.

Kealey, D. J., & Ruben, B. D. (1983). Cross-cultural personnel selection criteria, issues, and methods. In D. Landis & R. W. Brislin (Eds.), *Handbook of intercultural training* (pp. 155-175). Elmsford, NY: Pergamon.

Kelley, C., & Meyers, J. E. (1992a). *The Cross-Cultural Adaptability Inventory manual*. La Jolla, CA: C. Kelley & J. Meyers.

Kelley, C., & Meyers, J. E. (1992b). *The Cross-Cultural Adaptability Inventory: Action-planning guide*. La Jolla, CA: C. Kelley & J. Meyers.

Kluckhohn, F. R., & Strodtbeck, F. L. (1961). *Variations in value orientations*. New York: Row, Peterson.

Knight, E. M. (1981, February). *The case for teacher training in nonbiased, cross-cultural assessment*. Paper presented at the Council for Exceptional Children Conference on the Exceptional Bilingual Child, New Orleans.

Kobasa, S. C., Maddi, S. R., & Khan, S. (1983). Hardiness and health: A prospective study. *Journal of Personality and Social Psychology, 42,* 168-177.

Kobasa, S. C., Maddi, S. R., & Puccetti, M. C. (1982). Personality and exercise as buffers in the stress-illness relationship. *Journal of Behavioral Medicine, 5,* 391-404.

Kochman, T. (1981). *Black and white style in conflict and communication*. Chicago: University of Chicago Press.

Koester, J., & Olebe, M. (1988). The Behavioral Assessment Scale for intercultural communication effectiveness. *International Journal of Intercultural Relations, 12,* 233-246.

Kohls, R. L. (1984). *Survival kit for overseas living*. Yarmouth, ME: Intercultural Press.

Kristal, L., Pennock, P., Foote, S., & Trygstad, C. (1983). Cross-cultural family medicine residency training. *Journal of Family Practice, 17,* 683-687.

LaBrack, B. (Ed.). (1985). *The return home: A re-entry reader*. Stockton, CA: University of the Pacific, Office of International Programs.

Landis, D., & Brislin, R. (Eds.). (1983). *Handbook of intercultural training* (3 vols.). Elmsford, NY: Pergamon.

Landis, D., Brislin, R., & Hulgus, J. F. (1985). Attributional training versus contact in acculturative learning: A laboratory study. *Journal of Applied Social Psychology, 15,* 466-482.

Landis, D., Brislin, R., Swanner, G., Tzeng, O., & Thomas, J. (1985). Some effects of acculturative training: A field evaluation. *International Journal of Group Tensions, 15,* 68-91.

Landis, D., Day, H., McGrew, P., Miller, A., & Thomas, J. (1976). Can a black culture assimilator increase racial understanding? *Journal of Social Issues, 32,* 169-183.

Landis, D., & Tzeng, O. (1981). *Some effects of acculturative training: A field study*. Center for Applied Research and Evaluation Technical Report, Purdue University School of Science.

Landy, F. (1989). *Psychology of work behavior* (4th ed.). Belmont, CA: Wadsworth.

Laughlin, A. (1984). Teacher stress in an Australian setting: The role of biographical mediators. *Educational Studies, 10*(1), 7-22.

Lefley, H. (1984). Cross-cultural training for mental health professionals: Effects on the delivery of services. *Hospital and Community Psychiatry, 35,* 1227-1229.

Mabe, A. (1989). How do you teach world cultures? International students in the classroom. *Urban Anthropology and Studies of Cultural Systems and World Economic Development, 18,* 53-65.

Malinowski, B. (1927). *Sex and repression in savage society.* London: Humanities Press.

Malpass, R., & Salancik, G. (1977). Linear and branching formats in culture assimilator training. *International Journal of Intercultural Relations, 1,* 76-87.

Marquardt, M., & Hempstead, R. (1983). Training international officials in the U.S. *Training and Development Journal, 37*(10), 42-44.

Martin, J. (1986). Communication in the intercultural reentry: Student sojourners' perceptions of change in reentry relationship. *International Journal of Intercultural Relations, 10,* 1-22.

Maslow, A. H. (1954). *Motivation and personality.* New York: Harper & Row.

Mathison, S. (1991). What do we know about internal evaluation? *Evaluation and Program Planning, 14,* 159-165.

McGinnis, E., Goldstein, A. P., Sprafkin, R. P., & Gershaw, N. J. (1984). *Skillstreaming the elementary school child.* Champaign, IL: Research Press.

McShane, D. (1987). Mental health and North American Indian/native communities: Cultural transactions, education, and regulation. *American Journal of Community Psychology, 15,* 95-116.

Miller, K. (1989). Training peer counselors to work on a multicultural campus. *Journal of College Student Development, 30,* 561-562.

Montalvo, F., Lasater, T., & Valdez, N. (1982). Training child welfare workers for cultural awareness: The cultural simulator technique. *Child Welfare, 61,* 341-352.

Moyers, B. (1990). *A world of ideas: II.* Garden City, NY: Doubleday.

Naotsuka, R., Sakamoto, N., et al. (1981). *Mutual understanding of different cultures.* Tokyo: Taisukan.

Oberg, K. (1960). Cultural shock: Adjustment to new cultural environments. *Practical Anthropology, 7,* 177-182.

O'Brien, G. E., & Plooij, D. (1976). Development of cultural training manuals for medical workers with Pitjantjatjara aboriginals. In G. E. Kearney & D. W. McElwain (Eds.), *Aboriginal cognition: Retrospect and prospect* (pp. 383-396). Atlantic Highlands, NJ: Humanities Press.

O'Brien, G. E., Fiedler, F. E., & Hewett, T. (1970). The effects of programmed culture training upon the performance of volunteer medical teams. *Human Relations, 24,* 209-231.

Paige, M. (Ed.). (1992). *Education for the intercultural experience.* Yarmouth, ME: Intercultural Press.

Parker, W. M., Valley, M. M., & Geary, C. A. (1986). Acquiring cultural knowledge for counselors in training: A multi-faceted approach. *Counselor-Education-and-Supervision, 26,* 61-71.

Paunonen, S., Jackson, D. Trzebinski, J., & Forsterling, F. (1992). Personality structure across cultures: A multimethod evaluation. *Journal of Personality and Social Psychology, 62,* 447-456.

Pedersen, P. (1988). *A handbook for developing multicultural awareness.* Alexandria, VA: American Association for Counseling and Development.

Prothro, E. T. (1955). Arab-American differences in the judgment of written messages. *The Journal of Social Psychology, 42,* 3-11.

Ptak, C., Cooper, J., & Brislin, R. (1994). *Advice and insights for cross-cultural training programs as seen by experienced professional/"mentors."* Manuscript submitted for publication.

Randolph, G., Landis, D., & Tzeng, O. (1977). The effects of time and practice upon culture assimilator training. *International Journal of Intercultural Relations, 1,* 105-119.

Redick, L. T., & Wood, B. (1982). Cross-cultural problems for Southeast Asian refugee minors. *Child Welfare, 61,* 365-373.

Reitz, H., & Manning, M. (1994). *The one-stop guide to workshops.* New York: Irwin.

Rippert-Davila, S. (1985). Cross-cultural training for business: A consultant's primer. *The Modern Language Journal, 69,* 238-246.

Rokeach, M. (1979). *Understanding human values.* New York: Free Press.

Rossi, P., & Freeman, H. (1989). *Evaluation: A systematic approach* (4th ed.). Newbury Park, CA: Sage.

Ruben, B. D., & Kealey, D. J. (1979). *Behavioral assessment of communication competency and the prediction of cross-cultural adaption.* Ottawa: Canadian International Development Agency.

Runion, K., & Gregory, H. (1984). Training Native Americans to deliver mental health services to their own people. *Counselor Education and Supervisors, 23,* 225-233.

Sakamoto, N., & Naotsuka, R. (1982). *Polite fictions: Why Japanese and Americans seem rude to each other.* Tokyo: Kinseido.

Samovar, L., & Porter, R. (1991). *Intercultural communications: A reader* (6th ed.). Belmont, CA: Wadsworth.

Schneier, C., Guthrie, J., & Olian, J. (1988). A practical approach to conducting and using the training needs assessment. *Public Personnel Management, 17,* 191-205.

Schwartz, S. (1990). Individualism-collectivism: Critique and proposed refinements. *Journal of Cross-Cultural Psychology, 21,* 139-157.

Segall, M., Dasen, P., Berry, J., & Poortinga, Y. (1990). *Human behavior in global perspective.* Elmsford, NY: Pergamon.

Shibusawa, T., & Norton, J. (1989). *The Japan experience: Coping and beyond.* Tokyo: The Japan Times.

Silberman, M. (1990). *Active training.* Lexington, MA: Lexington.

Smith, J. C. (1985). *Relaxation dynamics: Nine world approaches to self-relaxation.* Champaign, IL: Research Press.

Spivak, G., Platt, J., & Shure, M. (1976). *The problem-solving approach to adjustment.* San Francisco: Jossey-Bass.

Steinkalk, E., & Taft, R. (1979). The effect of a planned intercultural experience on the attitudes and behaviors of the participants. *International Journal of Intercultural Relations, 3,* 187-197.

Sue, D. W., Bernier, J. E., Durran, A., Feinberg, L., Pedersen, P., Smith, C. J., & Varquez-Nuttall, G. (1982). Cross-cultural counseling competencies. *The Counseling Psychologist, 19*(2), 45-52.

Swierczek, F., & Carmichael, L. (1985). Assessing training needs: A skills approach. *Public Personnel Management, 14,* 259-274.

Triandis, H., Bontempo, R., Betancourt, H., & Bond, M., et al. (1986). The measurement of etic aspects of individualism and collectivism across cultures. *Australian Journal of Psychology, 38,* 257-267.

Triandis, H., Brislin, R., & Hui, C.H. (1988). Cross-cultural training across the individualism-collectivism divide. *International Journal of Intercultural Relations, 12,* 269-289.

Trifonovitch, G. (1977). On cross-cultural orientation techniques. In R. Brislin (Ed.), *Culture learning: Concepts, applications, and research* (pp. 213-222). Honolulu: University Press of Hawaii.

Trost, A. (1985). They may love it but will they use it? *Training and Development Journal, 39*(1), 78-81.

Ueda, K. (1974). Sixteen ways to avoid saying "no" in Japan. In J. Condon & M. Saito (Eds.), *Intercultural encounters with Japan* (pp. 185-192). Tokyo: The Simul Press.

Uehara, A. (1986). The nature of American student reentry adjustment and perceptions of the sojourn experience. *International Journal of Intercultural Relations, 10,* 415-438.

Useem, J., & Useem, R. (1967). The interface of a binational third culture: A study of the American community in India. *Journal of Social Issues, 23*(1), 130-143.

Useem, R. H. (1973, September). [comments on Third Culture Kids]. In *Overseas Educator* (A publication of the Office of International Extension, Michigan State University).

Wade, P., & Bernstein, B. (1991). Culture sensitivity training and counselor's race: Effects on black female clients. *Journal of Counseling Psychology, 38,* 9-15.

Walton, S. (1990). Stress management training for overseas effectiveness. *International Journal of Intercultural Relations, 14,* 507-527.

Waters, H. (1990). Preparing the African-American student for cooperate success: A focus on cooperative education. *International Journal of Intercultural Relations, 14,* 365-376.

Webb, M. (1990). Multicultural education in elementary and secondary schools. *ERIC Digest Number 67* (ED 327613).

Weick, K. (1984). Small wins: Redefining the scale of social problems. *American Psychologist, 39,* 40-49.

Weldon, D. E., Carlston, D. E., Rissman, A. K., Slobodin, L., & Triandis, H. C. (1975). A laboratory test of effects of culture assimilator training. *Journal of Personality and Social Psychology, 32,* 300-310.

Westwood, M., & Barker, M. (1990). Academic achievement and social adaption among international students: A comparison groups study of the peer-pairing program. *International Journal of Intercultural Relations, 14,* 251-263.

Whiting, R. (1989). *You gotta have wa.* New York: Vintage.

Williams, C. (1985). The Southeast Asian refugees and community mental health. *Journal of Community Psychology, 13,* 258-269.

Wood, P., & Mallinckrodt, B. (1990). Culturally sensitive assertiveness training for ethnic minority clients. *Professional Psychology Research and Practice, 21*(1), 5-11.

Worchel, S., & Mitchell, T. R. (1972). An evaluation of the effectiveness of the culture assimilator in Thailand and Greece. *Journal of Applied Psychology, 56,* 472-479.

Wurzel, J. (1983). Differences between Puerto Rican and Anglo-American secondary school students in their perception of relational modalities. *International Journal of Intercultural Relations, 17,* 181-190.

Zuker, E. (1989). *Mastering assertiveness skills.* New York: American Management Association.

Author Index

Subject Index

About the Authors

Richard W. Brislin is a Senior Fellow and Director of Intercultural Programs at the East-West Center in Honolulu. He received his Ph.D. in psychology from the Pennsylvania State University in 1969. He coordinates yearly programs at the East-West Center for college professors who want to integrate cross-cultural and intercultural research into their teaching; and for community leaders who offer various types of intercultural training workshops. He is the author or coauthor of a number of widely used books: *Cross-Cultural Research Methods* (1973); *Cross-Cultural Encounters: Face-to-Face Interaction* (1981); *Intercultural Interactions: A Practical Guide* (1986); and *Understanding Culture's Influence on Behavior* (1993). One of his recent books, *The Art of Getting Things Done: A Practical Guide to the Use of Power* (1991), was a selection of the Book of the Month Club and of the Quality Paperback Book Service. He was a G. Stanley Hall Lecturer for the American Psychological Association in 1987.

Tomoko Yoshida is the Director of Training for Japanese Programs, ITT Sheraton Hotels (Hawaii/Japan Division) in Honolulu. Prior to accepting this position, she was a project fellow at the East-West Center in Honolulu (1991-1992). She received her B.A. degree from International Christian University in Tokyo, Japan; and her M.S. in Counselor Education from Syracuse University in New York. While at the East-West Center, she served on the staff for workshops designed to assist college professors and community leaders increase their skills in offering various types of intercultural training courses and programs. In addition to her current work within the tourism industry, she has also directed workshops for cross-cultural counselors, merchants involved in retail sales, elementary school teachers, and journalists. She is coeditor of a recent book published by Sage: *Improving Intercultural Interactions: Modules for Cross-Cultural Training Programs* (1994). She has lived in the Philippines, Japan, the United States, and New Zealand.